Spotlight SCIENCE 7

★ Keith JOHNSON   ★ Gareth WILLIAMS
★ Sue ADAMSON   ★ Lawrie RYAN

With the active support of: Bob Wakefield, Anne Goldsworthy, Roger Frost, Helen Davis, Valerie Wood-Robinson, Phil Bunyan, Michael Cotter, Cathryn Mellor, John Bailey, Janet Hawkins, Ann Johnson, Graham Adamson, Diana Williams.

FRAMEWORK EDITION

First published in 2003 by:
Nelson Thornes Ltd
Delta Place
27 Bath Road
CHELTENHAM
GL53 7TH
United Kingdom

03 04 05 06 07 / 10 9 8 7 6 5 4 3 2 1

A catalogue record for this book is available from the British Library

ISBN 0 7487 7472 6

Illustrations by Jane Cope, Angela Lumley and Peters & Zabransky
Page make-up by Tech-Set

Printed and bound in Italy by Canale

Acknowledgements

The authors and publishers are grateful to the following for permission to reproduce photographs:

Ace Picture Library: 48T Laszlo Willinger, 95M Take Stock; Action Plus: 48BR; Adams Picture Library: 76BR; Alamy Images: 78T N Francis Robert Harding Picture Library, 78CB Joe Outland; Allsport: 175T Paul Severn; Ancient Art & Architecture Photolibrary: 175B; Ann Ronan: 53; Ardea: 42CR I R Beames, 45T C & J Knights; Associated Press: 163T Becker & Bredel; Axon Images: 54, 69, 74BR, 86ML, MR, 107ML, 111TL, 113BL; Biophoto Associates: 13, 52c, 56f, BOC Group: 101M; Bridgeman Art Library: 147; Bruce Coleman: 24BR Staffan Widstrand, 36BL J R Anthony, 46T Chris Gomersall, 56j M P L Fogden, 58BL Alain Compost, 59CR Hans Reinhard, 16C, 18T, BL, 162B; Bubbles Photolibrary: 113ii; CEFIC: 65B; Chris Fairclough Colour Library: 46B; Collections: 28T, 31TR, CR, 34 Anthea Sieveking, 101BR; Corel (NT): 16T, 18BR, 20T, 36T, BC, 45BR, 56g, 59BL, BR, 60, 67L, R, 72T, 74TR, 86BL, BR, 92TR, BL, BC, 107TL, 153, 161CR; Cotswold Wildlife Park: 58TL, CL, CR; Diamar (NT): 85; Digital Vision (NT): 61B, 166BR, 168; Ecoscene: 51B Griniewicz; Eric Crichton: 63; Frank Lane Picture Agency: 24BL Mark Newman, 51MR Michael Rose, 62 W Wisniewski, 52b; Geoscience Features Picture Library: 117B, 127BR, 128; Getty Images: 106TR Francesco Ruggeri/Image Bank, 116B Richard Kaylin/Stone, 178B Jon Gray/Stone; Glaxosmithkline: 70; Heinz: 86BCR; Holt Studios International: 21B N Cattlin; ICI: 84, 91, 106TL, B, 107TR; Impact Photos: 76TL,TR Alain Le Garsmeur; Israeli Tourist Office: 148; Jane Burton: 39T; Jean Francois Causse: 122; Jean-Mark Truchet: 149R; John Allen Cash: 42TCR, 43, 52e, 95TR, 126T, 132TL, 132TR; John P Carter: 145; John Walmesley Photography: 31CL, 135inset; J W Banagan: 138; Keith Johnson: 177; Klinge Chemicals: 107B Lo Salt is a registered trademark of Klinge Chemicals Ltd; Lisa Valder: 25, 31TL; London Fire Brigade: 141; Mahaux Photography: 129; Martyn Chillmaid: 4, 6T, 6B, 7, 9, 11T, 19T, 21T, 33, 48BL, 49, 51T, 64L, R, 65T, 66, 72B, 78CT, B, 80T, B, 86TL, TR, MC, 88, 90, 94TL, TCL, TCR, 95BR, BL, 96TL, TR, BL, BR, 97T, M, 98, 100L, 101BL, BC, 104L, 104R, 105, 107MR, 109, 110, 111TL, ML, MR, B, 113i, iii, iv, BR, 114T, B, 115B, T, 116a, c, d, e, f, g, 117T, 118T, 118T, M, 131, 134, 150, 156T, 171, 178T, 180, 186L, 186R; Mary Evans Picture Library: 132BL Barnaby's; Milepost 9½: 96TC British Rail Archive; NASA: 167MR ESA Meteosat, 119R, 162TR, 165, 166TL, 167TR, B, 170; Natural History Photographic Agency: 36BR Agence Nature; Natural Visions: 24TC, TR Heather Angel, 42TR, BR, 56b, c, 161L, CL, R; Oxford Scientific Films: 11B, 56e London Scientific Films, 16BL, 17T, 56h, k G I Bernard, 17B, 19B Manfred P Kage, 24TL Mark Stouffer, 24BC Alan Root, 39B Mark Ulrich, 50B Paul Franklin, 51ML Terry Button, 56a Roger Jackson, d David Thompson, 56i Alastair Shay, 59TL Mike Birkhead, 59CC, 187 Michael Fogden, 61T J A L Cooke, 103 Harold Taylor, 42TCL, BL, 45BL, 52a, d, 132BR; Panasonic UK: 176; Panos Pictures: 126B Glenn Edwards, 127BL Sean Sprague; Peter Fraekel: 127M; Photodisc (NT): 42TL, 44, 58TR, 74TL, 86BCL; Photographers Library: 76BL, 94TR; Planet Earth Pictures: 40; Popperfoto: 95BC, 99; Proctor & Gamble: 86TC; Professional Sport: 119L; Renshaw Scott Foods: 118B; Rex Features: 120 Today; Robert Harding Picture Library: 31B Patrick Ramsey, 135 Michael J Howell, 50T, 97B; Ron Sutherland: 23; Science & Society Picture Library: 83; Science Photolibrary: 12T Bruce Iverson, 12B Andrew Syred, 16BR P S U Entomology, 22 Chuck Brown, 26L, R, 28CL, CR, B, page 190 Petit Format Nestle, 27 Don Fawcett, 30 Katrina Thomas, 95TL R Folwell, 101T, 163B Adam Hart-Davis, 152T David Scharf, 160, 162TL John Sanford, 166TR, 167TR, ML NASA, 166BL Martin Dohrn, , 20B, 117M, 159, 167TL; Science Museum: 10; Sea Life Holdings Centre: 58BR; Stockmarket ZEFA: 92BR; T Hill: 107c; Timothy Woodcock Photolibrary: 152B; Tony Duffy: 73; Transport Research Laboratory: 156B; VARTA: 136; Viewfinder: 76BC; Wilderness Photographic: 125 John Noble; ZEFA-Kalt: 38a, b, c, d; Picture research by johnbailey@axonimages.com

Contents

How do detectives **investigate** a murder? They look for clues and then see what the clues mean.

We do this in science. We investigate by asking questions and looking for clues. We collect evidence and then we try to work out what the evidence means. We look for patterns in the evidence.

To investigate you need to use some basic skills. This introduction helps you with these skills. One of these skills is **observing**. (There is more about the skills we use in Science on page 171.)

Observing

▶ Are you a good observer? Try closing your eyes and counting how many things you can remember about this room.

▶ Now look carefully round the room. How many unusual things can you see?

Are there any notices on the walls? What do they say?

Is there any fire-fighting equipment? Why is it in that position?

How many hidden objects can you find?

▶ Your teacher will give you some **safety glasses**. Look at them carefully. How are they designed to protect your eyes?

Are they clean? If not, what should you do?

Keep them on until you are used to them. Remember your eyes can be easily damaged. Just think how your life would change if you were blind!

Look at the safety triangle sign. This sign is used to warn you of a possible danger! Whenever you see it, make sure you know what you must do to work safely.

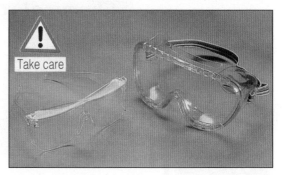

Your teacher will give your group a test-tube and a small piece of a chemical.

Put some water in the test-tube (about three-quarters full).

When your group is ready, drop the chemical into the water and observe it carefully. Write down or draw everything that happens. These are your **observations**.

When the experiment has finished, discuss your observations with each other.
Do you agree on everything that you saw? If not, what should you do now?

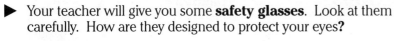

Report   (date)

What we did:

First we put some water in the test-tube (about ¾ full). Then

What we saw: (include a diagram)

► Look at the cartoon below, and discuss it in your group.

How many **un**safe things can you observe? Ten?

For each one, write down why it is unsafe and what **should** be done to make it safe.

Unsafe thing	Why is it unsafe?	What should be done?

1 Each science lab usually has a set of rules (a sort of Highway Code). Find the rules for your lab.
Read them and then write down the **reason** for having each rule.

2 Draw a safety poster for your science lab. Concentrate on one of the rules, and think how to get your message across clearly.

3 Look around your home, searching for unsafe situations where accidents might happen. Draw up a list.
Talk to your family about anything that should be made safer.

4 Draw a safety poster for your home.

5 Imagine you have a pen-pal in your last school. Write a letter telling her or him how you feel about today's science lesson.

Things to do

Observing

Learn about:
- observing in Science
- using a Bunsen burner

Observing is an important skill in science.
It helps you to be *scientific*.

▶ Are you observant? Write down (if you can):
- the colour of the paint in your bedroom
- the colour of the school gates
- the shape of the school gates
- the number or name on the door of this room.

▶ Look at the photographs. Can you identify them?
Write down the name of each object.

Good observers use *all* their senses, not just their eyes.

▶ Close your eyes and *listen* – how many different sounds can you identify?

Imagine eating a packet of crisps with your eyes shut.
What observations could you make? Make a list.

Place a candle so that everyone in your group can observe it.
Before you light it, think about *safety*: what needs to be done?

Then light the wick and observe the flame.

Write down as many observations as you can (about the flame, the candle and the wick).

Draw a labelled diagram of the candle and flame.
On your diagram, label something which is **solid**.
Then label something which is **liquid**.
Then label something which is not solid or liquid, but is a **gas**.

What can you observe when you blow out the candle?
Try to describe the smell.

The Bunsen burner

▶ Look at a Bunsen burner carefully.
How many parts has it got?

Where does the gas come in?

How can you change the size of the air-hole?

▶ Follow these instructions to light a Bunsen burner:

1. Put your Bunsen burner on a heat-proof mat.
2. Push the rubber tube firmly on to the gas-tap.
3. Close the air-hole.
4. Put on your safety glasses and keep them on. ⚠
5. Get a 'light', turn the gas-tap and light the burner.
6. Open the air-hole slowly and observe the changes in the flame.

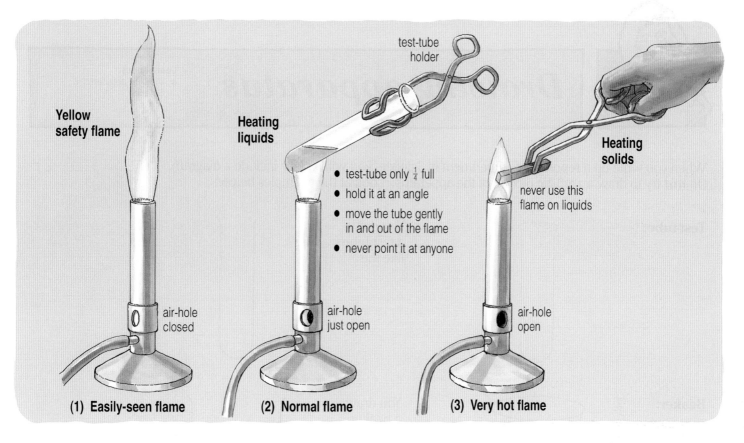

Yellow safety flame

air-hole closed

(1) Easily-seen flame

Heating liquids

test-tube holder

- test-tube only ¼ full
- hold it at an angle
- move the tube gently in and out of the flame
- never point it at anyone

air-hole just open

(2) Normal flame

Heating solids

never use this flame on liquids

air-hole open

(3) Very hot flame

a Which flame should you use when you are not heating anything?
b Why is this called the safety flame?
c Which flame will you use most often for heating?
d Why should you always wear safety glasses when using a Bunsen burner?

Get a short piece of magnesium ribbon from your teacher. Hold it at arm's length in some tongs. Then move it into the flame (do not look directly at it). What happens? What is left?

Where is magnesium used: • on November 5th?
                          • near a sinking ship?

Do you think a candle flame is as hot as a Bunsen flame?
How could you use two pieces of magnesium ribbon to test this?

Magnesium in action

1 Draw a diagram of a Bunsen burner and label it.
Where do you think the flame is hottest?

2 Explain:
a) how to light a Bunsen burner
b) how to get a normal heating flame
c) how to get an easily-seen flame
d) how to get a smaller flame
e) how to get a very hot flame.

3 A chip-pan fire in your kitchen is very dangerous. If it ever happens, why should you **not** throw water on it?
Why should you get hold of a wet towel and what should be done with it?

4 Write a short poem about flames.

5 Who was Robert Wilhelm Bunsen? Where did he live, and when? (He lost an eye because he didn't use safety glasses!)

Things to do

Drawing apparatus

When you write up a report of an experiment in Science, you will usually include a diagram.
Do **not** try to draw an artistic picture of the apparatus. Look at the examples below:

Test-tube:

You draw
a test-tube
like this:

Beaker:

You draw
a beaker
like this:

Conical flask:

You draw
a conical flask
like this:

Tripod and gauze:

You draw
a tripod and
gauze like this:

×××××××××××××

Remember: Always use a pencil for your drawings, and then use a pen to write the labels.
(You don't have to label common apparatus, such as the examples shown above.)

All living things are made up of building blocks called cells.

Cells make up tissues, tissues make up your organs and your organs make up you!

When male and female sex cells join together they make a new individual.

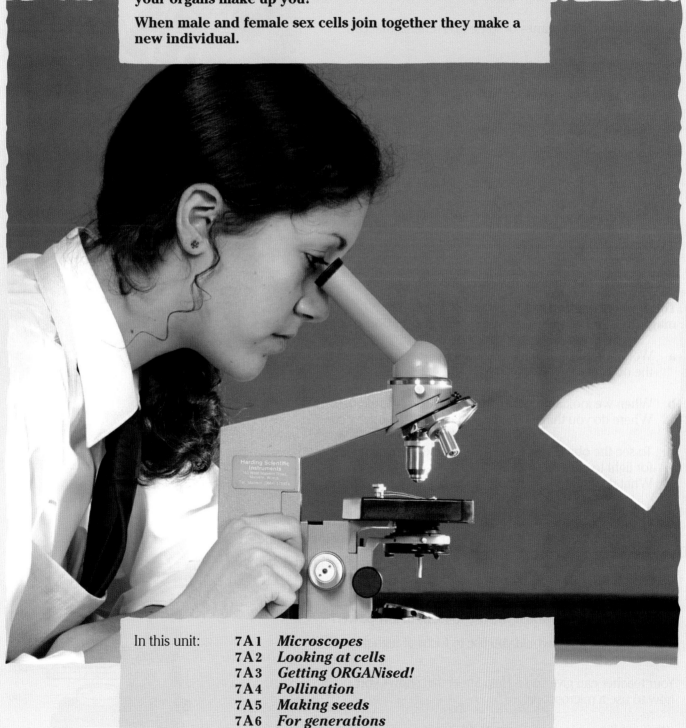

In this unit:

Microscopes

Learn about:
● using a microscope
● making drawings of objects viewed

Scientists study living things in great detail.
To observe them closely, they have to make their parts look bigger.
We say that they *magnify* them.

▶ Write down the names of some instruments that can magnify things.

What corking cells!

In 1665, Robert Hooke was using one of the first **microscopes**. It had two lenses instead of just one.

He looked down his microscope at a thin layer of cork.
He was able to see and draw what looked like tiny rooms.
Hooke called them **'cells'**.

▶ Look at a modern microscope.

Can you see that it has two lenses: the eyepiece lens and the objective lens?

If you look at the side of the lens it will tell you how much it magnifies.

You can work out the total magnification of an object.

**Total magnification =
magnification of eyepiece lens × magnification of objective lens**

An early microscope

a Work out the total magnification if the eyepiece lens is ×10 and the objective lens is ×10.

b When we look at a specimen we place it on a microscope slide. Where do you think the slide is placed on the microscope?

c To see the object under the microscope, it must be thin enough for light to pass through it.
What do you think the mirror is for?

d You can use low-power and high-power objective lenses.

   i) Which objective lens would you use to see most of the specimen?

   ii) Which objective lens would you use to see things in great detail?

e There are coarse and fine focussing knobs.

   i) Which knob would you use to focus at low power?

   ii) Which knob would you use to focus at high power?

Your teacher can give you a Help Sheet that shows you how to use a microscope.

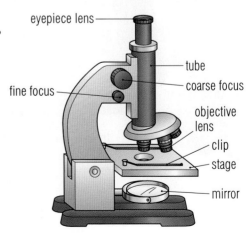

eyepiece lens — tube — coarse focus — fine focus — objective lens — clip — stage — mirror

Looking at specimens under the microscope

You can make microscope slides of lots of things.
Try some of these: newsprint, tissue paper, a hair, sand grains.

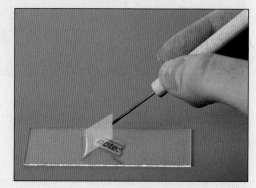

Put the specimen on to a microscope slide and add a drop of water.

Gently lower a cover-slip on to the slide using a mounted needle.

Place the slide on to the stage of the microscope.

Make sure that the mirror is directing light up through the slide.

Use a low-power objective and coarse focus to view the slide.

Turn on to the high-power objective lens and re-focus to see more detail.

Observing and drawing

Drawing **what you see** under the microscope is an important skill.

The photomicrograph shows some plant cells:

To draw a good diagram of this you need to:

- Make sure that your drawing fills about half a page.
- Use a sharpened HB pencil and have an eraser handy.
- Use clear clean lines for your drawing.
- Avoid shading and the use of coloured pencils.
- Draw only what you can see in the specimen.
- Use labels and clear label-lines around the drawing.
- Calculate the total magnification and write it on your drawing.

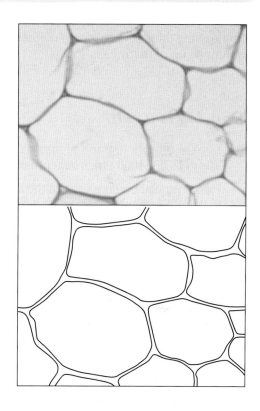

---

1 Copy and complete:
The total magnification is the . . . . of the eyepiece . . . . multiplied by the magnification of the . . . . lens. When we look at a . . . . we place it on a microscope . . . . which we then place on the . . . . of the microscope. The mirror is used to . . . . light up through the specimen. At low . . . . we focus using the . . . . focussing knob. At . . . . power we focus using the fine focussing knob.

2 a) What do we mean by magnification?
b) The eyepiece lens is ×10 and the total magnification is 400. What is the magnification of the objective lens?

3 Here are some instruments that let us observe things more closely:
a) telescope   c) endoscope
b) stethoscope   d) oscilloscope.
Find out what they are used for.

4 Find out more about the life and work of either
a) Robert Hooke or
b) Anton van Leeuwenhoek (who invented the first microscope) using books, ROMs or the internet.

Things to do

Looking at cells

Learn about:
- animal and plant cell differences
- cell parts and their functions
- cell adaptations

What is a cell?

Cells are the 'building blocks of life'.
Houses are made up of bricks stuck together.
Plants and animals are built up of cells stuck together.

With the help of a microscope you will be able to see cells.

All living things are made up of cells.
Some living things are made up of just one cell, but most
are made up of many cells.

How big is a cell?

▶ Look at this photograph of human cheek cells:
The cells are 1000 times larger than in real life.

Plan how you could work out the actual size of one of the cells
in the photograph. Then work it out.

It's a fact!

Your body probably contains about a million
million cells!

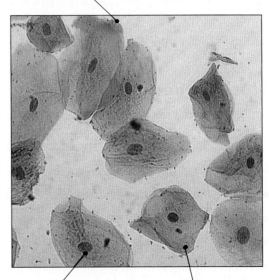

cell membrane: contains the cell
and controls what passes in and
out of the cell

nucleus: controls the cell
and contains instructions
to make more cells

cytoplasm: where the
chemical reactions of
the cell take place
to keep the cell alive

Looking at plant cells

Make a slide of a thin piece of onion skin.

Look at it under the microscope at low power.
What do you see?

Now look at the cells under the microscope
at high magnification.

Your onion cells look different from the cheek cells shown above.

All plant cells have:

- a box-like shape

- a thick **cell wall** around the outside to support the cell

- a **vacuole** containing a watery solution called **cell sap**.

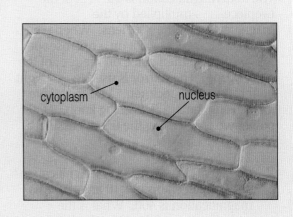

cytoplasm   nucleus

Looking at chloroplasts

Chloroplasts are very small structures that are found in many plant cells. They contain **chlorophyll** which traps light energy. This energy helps plants to make their own food. This process is called **photosynthesis**.

Why are there no chloroplasts in onion cells?

Make a slide of a moss leaf.

Look at the cells under the microscope at high magnification. Can you see the chloroplasts?

Make a large drawing of 2 or 3 cells. Label the parts.

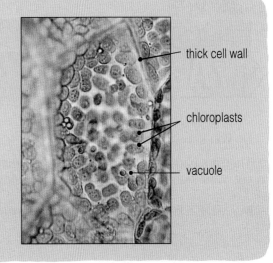

- thick cell wall
- chloroplasts
- vacuole

Special cells

Lots of cells in plants and animals have changed their shape to do a particular job.

Look at these cells:

▶ In the table below the shapes of these cells and the jobs that they do are all jumbled up.

Copy out the table putting in the correct shape and job for each cell.

Type of cell	Shape	Job
sperm cell	hollow tube	carries oxygen
xylem cell	wire-like	swims to the egg
red blood cell	has a tail	carries water
nerve cell	flat disc	carries messages

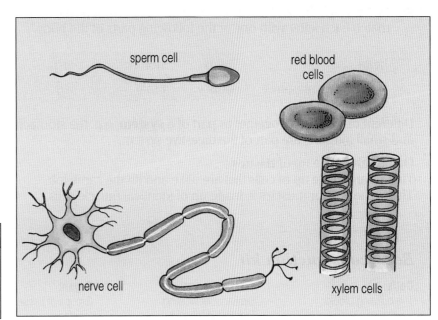

sperm cell

red blood cells

nerve cell

xylem cells

Things to do

1 Copy and complete this table.

	Cheek cell (animal)	Onion cell (plant)	Moss leaf cell (plant)
Does it have a nucleus?			
Does it have a cell wall?			
Does it have chloroplasts?			
Does it have a vacuole?			

2 Write down what you think each of the following cell parts do:
a) chloroplast
b) cell membrane
c) cell wall
d) nucleus.

3 The cells shown above are called **specialised cells**.
Use secondary sources of information (books, videos, ROMs and/or the internet), to find out about one other specialised cell. Explain how it is adapted for its function.

Getting ORGANised!

Learn about:
- cells, tissues and organs
- plant and animal tissues

Do you know what **organs** are?

They are parts of your body that do a particular job for you,
e.g. your kidneys get rid of waste and control your water balance.

▶ Make a list of some other organs in your body and say what they do.

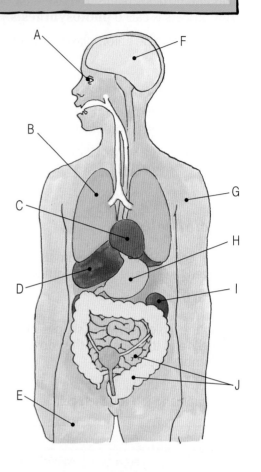

The see-through body

▶ Write down the letters A to J. Study the diagram opposite and match each letter with one of the following parts of the body:

heart	eye	lungs	stomach	arm
liver	intestines	kidney	brain	leg

Different organs work together as part of a **system**, e.g. the stomach and small intestine are part of the digestive system.

Organs are made up of **tissues**.
Tissues are made up of cells that are alike and do the same job.
The tissue in your muscles is made up of identical muscle cells.

Body construction kit

Cells:
The building blocks.

Tissue:
Similar cells working together in the same way.

Organ:
Groups of tissues working together.

System:
A group of organs working together.

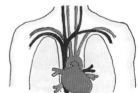

Muscle cells contract and relax.

Muscle tissue is made of muscle cells that contract and relax together.

Your heart is made up of muscle tissue. It pumps blood around your body.

Heart and blood vessels make up your **circulatory** system. The circulatory system carries blood around your body.

▶ Make a list of some types of cell found in your body and say what jobs they do.

It's a fact!

Most animals and plants have many different types of cells all doing different jobs. Your body has over 200 different types of cell!

The working plant

Plants have bodies too. They are also made up of many different organs, such as leaves, flowers and roots.

▶ Write down the letters A to F. Study this diagram and match each letter with one of the following parts of the plant:

| root | leaf | fruit | flower | bud | stem |

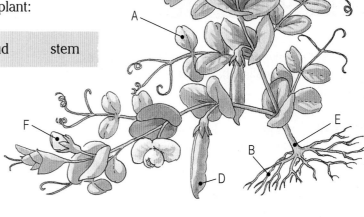

We can look at the organisation of a plant organ, the root, in more detail below:

Cells:

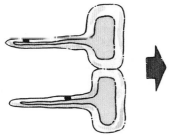

Root hair cells absorb water from the soil.

Tissue:

The root hairs pass water to the root cells.

Organ:

The root passes water into the stem.

System:

Water travels up the stem to the leaves.

---

1 Copy and complete:
A tissue is made up of . . . . that carry out the same . . . . An organ is formed from groups of . . . . working together. A . . . . is a group of organs working together.

2 Copy out the organs listed on the left. Match each with the correct system from those listed on the right.

Lungs and windpipe	Blood system
Heart and vessels	Nervous system
Brain and spinal cord	Breathing system
Kidneys and bladder	Digestive system
Stomach and intestines	Excretory system

3 Imagine that you are a particular organ in the body. Write about what you are like and what job you do in the body. Don't forget to say why you think you are so important.

4 Using a house as a model for an organism (living thing), explain how cells, tissues, organs and systems are organised.

Things to do

Pollination

Learn about:
- male and female sex cells in plants
- the process of pollination

Many people give flowers to friends and relatives. But how many realise that flowers are a plant's reproductive system?

Flowers have male and female reproductive organs. The male parts produce the male sex cells. The female parts produce the female sex cells.

▶ Write down some words to describe what flowers are like.

A closer look

You can use a hand-lens to look at your flower in more detail. Cut the flower in half like the one in the picture. See if you can find all the parts labelled in the picture.

Many flowers have male and female parts. The female parts are called the **carpels**. Look at the picture:

a What is each carpel made up of?

The male parts are called the **stamens**.

b What is each stamen made up of?

Use a hand-lens to look closely at these parts in your flower.

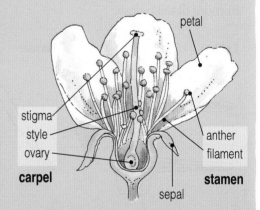

stigma
style
ovary
carpel
sepal
petal
anther
filament
stamen

Make a flower poster

Take a new flower and carefully remove all the parts with tweezers. Start on the outside with the sepals. Then work inwards removing the petals, stamens and carpels. Arrange the parts in a line, one under the other, in your book. Stick them down neatly with sellotape and label the parts. Your teacher can give you a Help Sheet that shows you how to do this.

Male and female cells

The stamens are the male parts of a flower. Each stamen is an **anther** and a **filament** (or stalk). The male sex cells are made inside the anthers. Each male sex cell is called a **pollen grain**.

The carpels are the female parts of a flower. Each carpel is made up of a **stigma**, a **style** and an **ovary**. The female sex cells are made inside the ovary. Each female sex cell is called an **ovule**.

If fertilisation is to take place, a pollen grain and an ovule must join together. Their cells each contain a nucleus with the information that is passed on from one generation to the next.

Can you see the ovary in this flower?

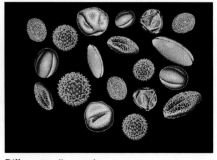

Different pollen grains

Carried by insects

Pollination is the transfer of pollen from the anthers of a flower to the stigma.

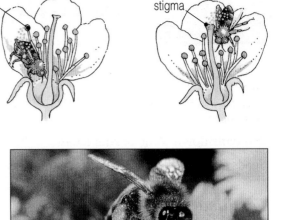

anther

stigma

c At what time of year are most flowers out?

d At what time of year are insects such as bees and butterflies out?

Insects are a great help in carrying pollen from one flower to another.
But first, the flowers have to attract the insects to them.

e Write down 3 ways in which flowers can attract insects.

▶ Look at the picture showing **insect pollination**.

f Why do you think the bee reaches down into the first flower?

g How does the bee carry pollen to the second flower?

h Where does the bee leave pollen in the second flower?

Blown by the wind

Not all flowers need insects to pollinate them.
Many flowers like grasses and cereals rely on the wind to carry their pollen to another flower.

▶ Look at a wind-pollinated flower with a hand-lens.

i How does it compare with your insect-pollinated flower?
  • Is it brightly coloured?
  • Does it have a scent?
  • Does it have **nectar**?

j Why do you think this is?

k What do you think its pollen is like?
  • Is the pollen sticky?
  • Is it light or heavy?
  • Is much pollen produced?

l Why do you think this is?

▶ Make a table to show all the differences that you have found out between insect-pollinated flowers and wind-pollinated flowers.

---

1 Copy and complete:
The male parts of a flower are called the . . . . and are made up of 2 parts: the . . . . and the . . . . The female parts of a flower are called the . . . . and are made up of the . . . . , the . . . . and the . . . . Pollination is the transfer of . . . . from the anthers of one flower to the . . . . of another.

2 **Cross-pollination** is when pollen is transferred to separate flowers. What do you think is meant by **self-pollination**? How could it take place?

3 Did you know that 1 in 10 people suffer from **hay fever**?
Find out what the symptoms are.
When do you think people suffer most?
Find out what the **pollen count** is and what sort of weather conditons can affect it.

4 Copy and complete these half-sentences:
a) Some flowers attract insects because they have . . . .
b) Wind-pollinated flowers do not need colour because . . . .
c) Insect-pollinated flowers have sticky pollen because . . . .
d) Wind-pollinated flowers make lots of pollen because . . . .

Things to do

Making seeds

Learn about:
● fertilisation in plants
● cell division and growth

Most new plants grow from **seeds**.
But where do you think seeds come from?
How are seeds formed?

▶ Write down some of your ideas.

Seeds are formed when a male sex cell joins with a female sex cell.

Fertilisation

Inside each pollen grain is a male **pollen nucleus**.
Inside each ovule is a female **ovule nucleus**.

a What do we call the joining together of a male nucleus and a female nucleus?

Once it is fertilised, the ovule grows into a seed.

▶ Look at the pictures to see how fertilisation takes place in a flowering plant:

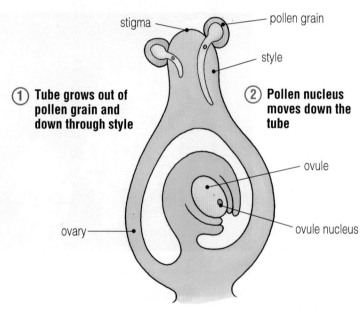

stigma — pollen grain

style

① **Tube grows out of pollen grain and down through style**

② **Pollen nucleus moves down the tube**

ovule

ovary

ovule nucleus

③ **Pollen nucleus joins with ovule nucleus. Fertilisation takes place and a seed will form.**

b Where do you think the pollen grain comes from?

c What happens to a pollen grain after it lands on a stigma?

d How does the pollen nucleus reach the ovule nucleus?

After fertilisation, most parts of the flower, wither and die.
The ovary gets bigger and forms the **fruit**. Inside the fruit are the seeds.

e What do you think the fruits and seeds are like in these plants:
   i) grape?   ii) oak tree?   iii) pea?   iv) tomato?

If a new plant is to survive and grow well its seed must first be carried away from the parent plant.
Seeds are often scattered over a wide area.

f Why do you think this is important?

g Write down some different ways in which seeds can be scattered.

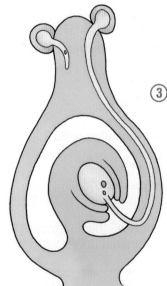

Pea and pod seeds

Half a tomato fruit: can you see the seeds?

Seed fall

"Seeds that fall slowly have a better chance of being carried further by the wind" said the man in the gardening programme.
Do you think that this is true?

Plan an investigation to find out how slowly different seeds fall.

- Think carefully about what apparatus you will need.
- What measurements are you going to make?
- Remember to make it a fair and safe test.

Show your plan to your teacher, then try it out.

Cell division

We grow when one cell divides to make 2 new cells.
The nucleus of the original cell contains the information needed to make the parts of the new cells.
The nucleus divides first passing information to each new cell.
Then the cytoplasm divides and the 2 cells separate.

h Draw some simple diagrams to show how you think one cell divides.

i How could one cell eventually make eight?

Once fertilisation has taken place, the fertilised egg cell divides to make new cells.

j Where does the information to make these new cells come from?

You can see the process of cell division taking place in these yeast cells:

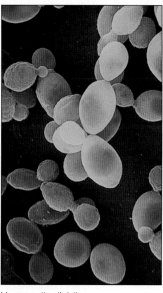

Yeast cells dividing

---

1 Write out the following sentences in the correct order to describe how plants reproduce:
A Pollen nucleus joins with ovule nucleus.
B Pollen grain lands on stigma.
C The fertilised ovule becomes a seed.
D The pollen grain grows into a pollen tube.
E The pollen nucleus travels down the pollen tube to the ovule.

2 What do we mean by fertilisation?
In a flowering plant, what takes the place of:
a) the sperm?   b) the egg?
c) the fertilised egg?

3 What happens to each of the following after fertilisation:
a) the flower?   b) the ovule?
c) the ovary?

4 a) Why don't seeds germinate (grow) in a gardening shop?
b) What do they need to grow?
c) Copy the drawing of a germinating seed and label it using these words:

> new leaves   seed coat   new root
> new shoot   food store

Things to do

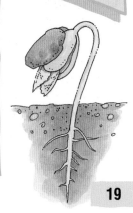

19

For generations

▶ Write down some ways in which plants can make new plants.

a What structures make up the reproductive systems of a plant?

The job of a flower is to make seeds which grow into new plants.

Pollen grains contain the male sex cells and the ovule contains the female sex cells. When they join together the fertilised ovule divides to make many cells that form the **embryo** (new plant).

b How does pollen get from one flower to another?

When pollen lands on a stigma of a similar flower it starts to grow a pollen tube.

c Why does the pollen grain need to grow a pollen tube?

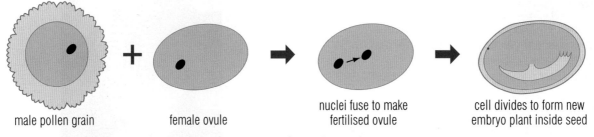

| male pollen grain | female ovule | nuclei fuse to make fertilised ovule | cell divides to form new embryo plant inside seed |

Half the information in the embryo plant comes from the male pollen nucleus and half comes from the female ovule nucleus.

Looking at the growth of pollen grains

The pollen grains in the photograph were scraped off the anthers of a flower with a mounted needle.
They were then placed on a microscope slide with a few drops of 10% sugar solution and a cover-slip put on the top.
The slide was placed in the dark for 2 hours.

After 2 hours, some pollen grains grew pollen tubes.

Plan an investigation to find out the best sugar concentration for pollen tube growth.

- What will be the title for your investigation?
- What range of sugar concentrations will you use?
- What variables will you try to keep the same?
- How many pollen grains will you use? 20 would be a good sample.
- How will you tell how many pollen grains have grown in your sample?
- How will you record your results?
- What graphs will you draw to show the data in your results?
  How will you identify any trends in your data?

Compare your graphs with other groups and evaluate the strength of your evidence.

Write an account of your investigation.

Different plant cells

The plant cell in the diagram is taken from a leaf:

It looks a lot different from a pollen grain.
It also looks a lot different from an animal cell.

d Make a list of the ways in which this plant cell is different from an animal cell.

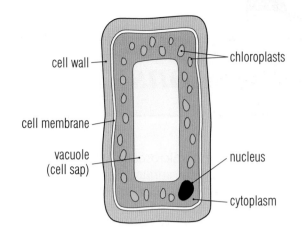

cell wall
chloroplasts
cell membrane
vacuole (cell sap)
nucleus
cytoplasm

Investigation: Beet this!

A beetroot is a plant organ that stores food over the winter.
In the spring the new plant uses this food for growth.
Beetroot tissue is made up of cells that contain a red dye.
This dye leaks out if the cells are put into hot water.

How can you get the most dye out of a chip of beetroot?

Plan your investigation.

Decide what apparatus you will need and how you are going to record your results.

Remember that it must be a fair test.

Show your plan to your teacher and then start your investigation.

Things to do

1 Copy and complete:
Pollen grains contain the . . . . sex cell and the . . . . contains the female sex cell. After pollination the male . . . . grain lands on the . . . . of another flower. The pollen grain germinates and forms a pollen . . . . which grows down the . . . . to the female ovule. Here the two sex cells join together to form an . . . . This is called . . . . You can get pollen grains to grow tubes by placing them in . . . . solution and observing them under the microscope.

2 Draw a flow diagram to show how a pollen grain nucleus gets from the anther to join with an ovule nucleus in the ovary of another flower.

3 Plants cells are not all alike. Copy and complete the table to show how the structure and the jobs of these plant cells is different (the first one has been done for you):

Plant cell	Where found	Structure	Job done
Xylem cell	stem, root and leaf	long, thin tubes	carries water and salts up to leaves
Leaf cell			
Root hair cell			
Pollen grain			

4 Imagine that you are a plant breeder and you want to produce the best possible plants for a British spring garden.
a) What sort of characters would you breed in to these plants?
b) How would you get the sex cells, with the information for these good characters, together?
c) How would you look after the new young plants that you have produced?

Questions

1 When using your microscope, why should you:
   a) never touch the surfaces of the lenses or mirror?
   b) put a cover-slip over what you want to observe on a slide?
   c) focus on low power first before turning up to high power?

2 Write a help card for next year's Year 7 classes showing them how to set up and view the cells in the skin of an onion.

3 Imagine that you are a pollen cell.
Describe your adventures on the way to fertilising an ovule.
You can choose to be from a wind- or insect-pollinated plant.

4 Make a list of all the specialised cells you have met in this topic.
Explain briefly how each one is adapted for its function.

5 Look carefully at this photograph of plant cells:
How many different types of cell can you see?
Describe or draw each different cell.
Why don't they all look the same?

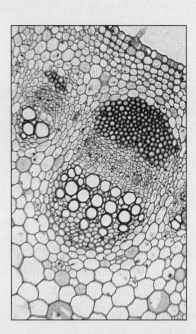

6 Try putting some celery into coloured water. You can colour the water with a little food colouring or ink. Leave your celery for a few hours and then look at it. The coloured lines are xylem.
What job do you think xylem does?
Which plant groups have xylem and which do not?

7 Cells can do different jobs.
Draw a cartoon character cell that does a particular job in the human body.
Write about what your cell would do in a typical day.

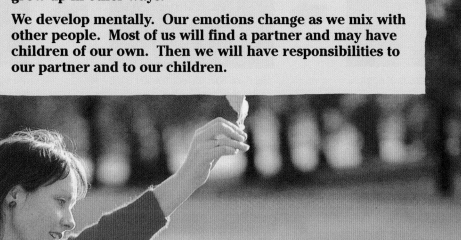

As we grow up, each of us changes from a baby to a child, then to a teenager and eventually to an adult.

But growing up doesn't just mean we get bigger. We also grow up in other ways.

We develop mentally. Our emotions change as we mix with other people. Most of us will find a partner and may have children of our own. Then we will have responsibilities to our partner and to our children.

Having babies

Learn about:
- the ways different animals reproduce and develop
- the human reproductive system

▶ Look at the photos showing how new life starts in two very different animals:

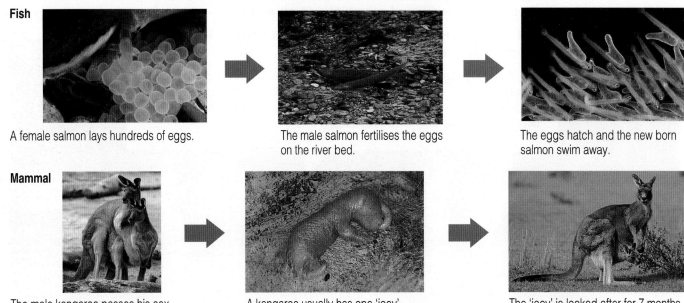

Fish

A female salmon lays hundreds of eggs.

The male salmon fertilises the eggs on the river bed.

The eggs hatch and the new born salmon swim away.

Mammal

The male kangaroo passes his sex cells into the female kangaroo when they mate.

A kangaroo usually has one 'joey'.

The 'joey' is looked after for 7 months in the mother's pouch.

▶ Discuss the differences between the salmon and the kangaroo, comparing:
  - how reproduction takes place
  - the number of offspring
  - the life of the newly-born animal
  - the rate of development of the young animal.

▶ Write down an explanation for the differences you have discussed above.

How are human babies made?

To start a baby the male and female sex cells must join together. A **sperm** from a man must join with an **egg** from a woman. This is called **fertilisation**. In humans it occurs inside the woman's body.

Here are the parts of a man that are used for making sperms:

▶ Your teacher will give you a copy of this diagram.

a Shade in blue where sperms are made.

b Shade in red where fluid is added to the sperms.

c Shade in yellow the tubes that the sperms pass through to get to the outside.

d List the parts that the sperms pass through.

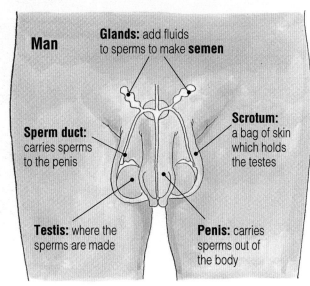

Man

Glands: add fluids to sperms to make **semen**

Sperm duct: carries sperms to the penis

Scrotum: a bag of skin which holds the testes

Testis: where the sperms are made

Penis: carries sperms out of the body

Here are the parts of a woman that are used to make eggs and produce babies:

▶ Your teacher will give you a copy of this diagram.

e Shade in blue where eggs are made.

f Shade in red where fertilisation may take place.

g Shade in yellow where the baby develops.

h List the parts that the egg would pass through on its way out of the body.

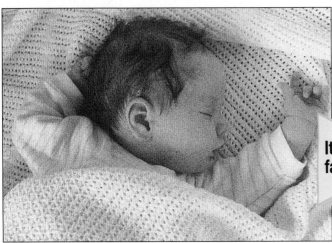

Woman

Uterus: in a pregnant woman the baby grows here

Oviduct (egg tube): carries the egg to the uterus every month

Ovaries: where the eggs are made

Cervix: the opening to the uterus

Vagina: receives the sperm

It's a fact!

When a girl is born she has thousands of partly-formed eggs in each ovary. When she grows into a woman an egg will be released from one of her ovaries about every 28 days.

▶ Copy out these sentences and add as much as you can, using words from the box opposite:

- I know that females have …
- I know that males have …
- Fertilisation is when …
- Babies grow …

Now make some sentences of your own using some of these words.

> testes   egg   uterus   sperms
>
> vagina   oviduct   sperm duct
>
> where eggs are made
>
> penis   ovaries   scrotum
>
> where sperms are made

Things to do

1 Copy out the words in the following list. If you think that they are female put (F) after them. If you think that they are male put (M).

ovaries	oviduct	penis
uterus	testes	vagina
scrotum	sperm duct	cervix

2 Sometimes a woman's oviducts get blocked.
a) Why do you think that a woman with both oviducts blocked cannot have a baby?
b) Why do you think that a woman with one oviduct blocked might be able to have a baby?

3 Copy out the list of organs on the left and match each organ with its correct job from the list on the right.

penis	carries sperms to penis
ovaries	where the baby grows
sperm duct	makes sperms
vagina	carries eggs to uterus
uterus	makes eggs
testes	receives sperms
oviduct	holds testes
scrotum	carries sperms out of body

4 Do some research to find out about reproduction and the early life of a frog or a seahorse.

Fertilisation

Learn about:
- fertilisation in humans
- the sperm and egg cells and their nuclei

▶ Look at these photographs of the human sperm and the human egg. Write down as many differences as you can between the sperm and the egg.

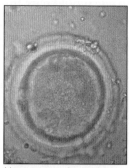 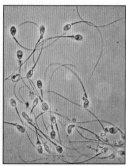

Human egg – its nucleus contains the female half of the information to be passed on from the mother

Human sperm – its nucleus contains the male half of the information from the father

Making love

When people 'make love' or 'have sex' it is not just so that they can have babies. Men and women can enjoy making love at other times too. They use it as a way of showing their love for each other. By having sex a man and woman can feel very close to each other. Making love is far more than putting a sperm and an egg together.

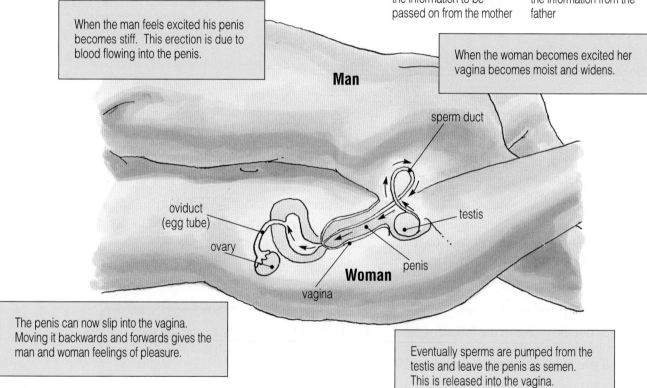

When the man feels excited his penis becomes stiff. This erection is due to blood flowing into the penis.

When the woman becomes excited her vagina becomes moist and widens.

Man

sperm duct

oviduct (egg tube)

ovary

testis

penis

Woman

vagina

The penis can now slip into the vagina. Moving it backwards and forwards gives the man and woman feelings of pleasure.

Eventually sperms are pumped from the testis and leave the penis as semen. This is released into the vagina.

▶ Write out the following statements. Put (T) for true after those you agree with and (F) for false after those you don't agree with.

People have sex because they want babies.

Fertilisation takes place in the oviduct (egg tube).

You have to be married to have sex.

During sex body fluids are released.

A sperm and an egg are not cells.

For sex to occur a man's penis must be hard.

Some people don't have sex (are virgins) all their life.

It's a fact!

Only about a teaspoonful of semen is released at a time, but this can contain as many as 500 million sperms.

After making love ...

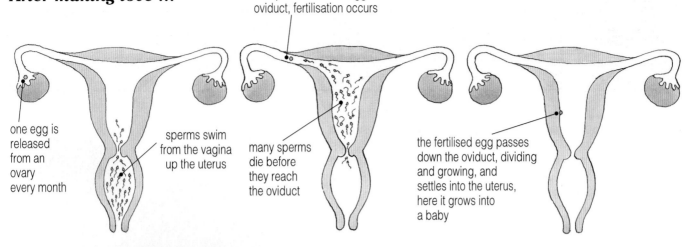

if a sperm meets an egg in the oviduct, fertilisation occurs

one egg is released from an ovary every month

sperms swim from the vagina up the uterus

many sperms die before they reach the oviduct

the fertilised egg passes down the oviduct, dividing and growing, and settles into the uterus, here it grows into a baby

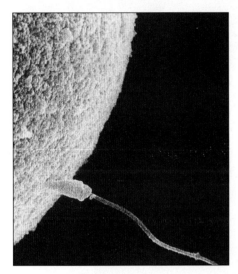

When the sperm meets the egg it loses its tail. The sperm head enters the egg and its nucleus fuses (joins) with the egg nucleus: this is **fertilisation**. The nucleus of the fertilised egg now contains the genetic information from the father and mother.

What do you think?

▶ In groups discuss these statements:

It is against the law to have sex under the age of 16.

Many people say that they have had sex when they haven't.

People should have sex only if they are in love with each other.

Men are more interested in sex than women.

Not too many

▶ Many societies have their own rules and traditions which help to stop too many children being born. Write about:

- what these rules and traditions are in *your* society
- how they help to control the growth of the population
- rules and traditions used in other countries.

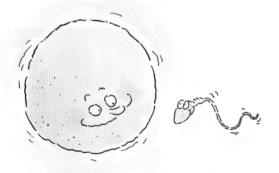

---

1 Copy out and complete the following sentences:
a) Fertilisation is the joining together of . . . .
b) The sperms are released into . . . .
c) To get to the oviduct, the sperms swim . . . .
d) An egg is released from an ovary every . . . .
e) The fertilised egg passes down the oviduct . . . .

2 a) What do you think might happen if the fertilised egg splits into two?
b) Find out how we can get non-identical twins.

3 Try to explain each of these statements:
a) Fish and frogs produce thousands of eggs into the water.
b) Humans usually produce one egg at a time inside the body of the woman.
c) Men produce millions of sperms.

Things to do

Ruth and Jim

Learn about:
● the development of the fetus
● the functions of the placenta
● how harmful substances can cross the placenta

Ruth and Jim had wanted a baby for a long time. When Ruth missed her period, they hoped she might be **pregnant**. Ruth went to see her doctor and took along a sample of her urine for a test. After a short time she was told that the test was positive – she was pregnant! She told Jim straight away. They were both so happy and excited at the thought of a baby after waiting for so long.

In the weeks that followed they started to make plans for the new baby. Ruth went to the **ante-natal clinic** regularly. The nurse asked her questions like:
Was it her first pregnancy?
Had she ever had any serious illnesses?
Had there been serious illnesses in her family or in Jim's?
Were there any twins in her family or in Jim's?

Whenever Ruth went to the clinic the nurse weighed her and measured her blood pressure. The midwife or doctor examined her on each visit and she was given lots of advice about how to prepare for the birth of her baby.

▶ Think about Ruth's visits to the ante-natal clinic and answer the following questions.

a Why do you think Ruth was asked about serious illnesses in the family?

b Why was she asked if there were twins in the family?

c Why do you think she was weighed?

d Why do you think her blood pressure was taken?

e Ruth doesn't smoke. Why might the nurse have been worried if she did?

A new life begins

When the fertilised egg passed down Ruth's oviduct it divided and grew. Then it settled in the thick wall of her uterus. As it grew there it eventually formed a **fetus** ('feet-us').

▶ Look at these photographs of the developing fetus inside the uterus:

f What changes can you see? Write them down.

Early in pregnancy, a plate-shaped organ called a **placenta** forms in the uterus. This acts as a barrier stopping infections and harmful substances from reaching the fetus. Inside the placenta the blood of the fetus and the mother come close together. The fetus is attached to the placenta by the **umbilical cord**.

▶ Write down your answers to these questions.

g How do you think food and oxygen get to the fetus?

h How do you think the fetus gets rid of waste?

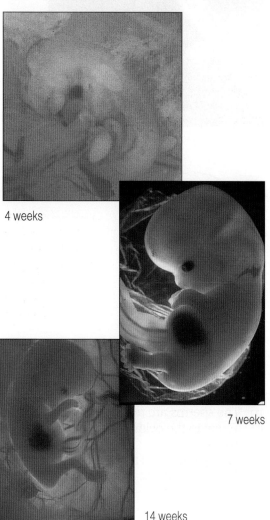

4 weeks

7 weeks

14 weeks

▶ Look at this diagram of the fetus inside the mother:

i How do you think it is protected during its development?

j Can you see that it is surrounded by a fluid? How do you think this helps the fetus?

Immature thoughts

▶ Imagine that you are inside the uterus before birth. What is it like?
How do you feed?
How do you breathe?
How are you protected from bumps?
What do you hear?

Write a short story about your experiences.

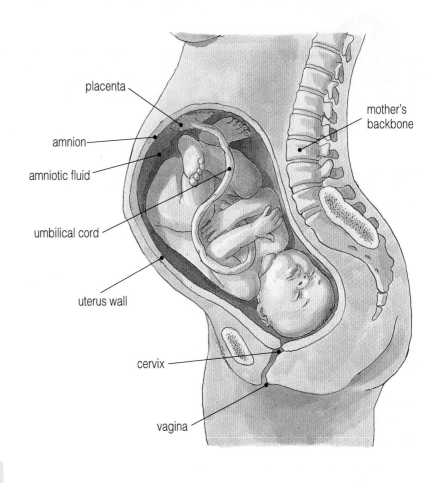

placenta

mother's backbone

amnion

amniotic fluid

umbilical cord

uterus wall

cervix

vagina

It's a fact!

The placenta can't act as a barrier to all harmful substances. In the 1960s the drug thalidomide was given to some pregnant women to help them sleep. Some of them gave birth to babies with no arms or legs.

Eating for two

The pregnant mother must eat sensibly. She may be 'eating for two' but that doesn't mean she has to eat twice as much! **Protein** is needed for the baby to grow. It will also need **calcium** for healthy bones and teeth, and **iron** to build up blood cells.

▶ In your groups, design a poster to show pregnant women that their habits, good and bad, will affect their babies.

It's a fact!

Some germs can get across the placenta to the fetus. If the mother has German measles it can affect the baby's eyes and heart and cause deafness. Twelve-year old girls are given a rubella injection to stop them catching German measles.

1 What important jobs do each of these do:
a) the placenta?
b) the umbilical cord?
c) the amnion?

2 What advice would you give to Ruth about keeping healthy during pregnancy? How could smoking and drinking alcohol affect her unborn baby?

3 Collect some leaflets or articles giving advice on pregnancy.
Make your own leaflets for an ante-natal clinic.

4 How do you think Jim could have helped Ruth during her pregnancy?
Find out by looking at leaflets and by asking some fathers.

Things to do

Birth and after

Learn about:
● the birth of a baby
● the needs of a new-born baby
● breast feeding

Think about what it is like to be a new-born baby.
How is life outside different from life inside the mother?

▶ Copy and complete this table:

	Inside the uterus	After the birth
How does the baby get food?		
How does the baby get oxygen?		
What sort of things does the baby react to?		
How is the baby protected?		

Ruth's baby

Ruth had been pregnant for 36 weeks.

One day she felt the muscles in her uterus squeezing (**contracting**).
This was the start of **labour**.

Jim took her to the hospital straight away.
He and the **midwife** helped her to get ready for the birth.
The midwife checked the size of the opening in Ruth's cervix.
It gradually gets wider in preparation for the birth.
Her contractions were getting stronger and coming more often.
Soon the sac of amniotic fluid around the baby broke.

After several hours of gradual pushing by Ruth, the baby was born.
It came out head first through her vagina. It was a girl!

She was still joined to Ruth by the umbilical cord. The doctor cut this.
Later the rest of the umbilical cord and the placenta came out.
This is called the **afterbirth**.

Ruth rested and the baby slept. Soon the baby was hungry.
She had milk for the baby from her breasts.
Ruth and Jim decided to call her Laura.

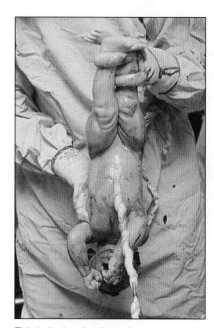

This baby has just been born.
The umbilical cord is about to be tied
and cut.

▶ Write down your answers to the following questions.

a How did the baby come out of Ruth's body?

b What was the umbilical cord for?

c Where was your cord joined to your body at birth?

d What is the afterbirth?

Looking after baby

Humans take care of their babies.

▶ When you were a baby you needed things to make you feel happy and safe. You also needed things in order to grow and keep healthy.

Make a list of the things you needed.

Babies have:
- **physical** needs, like warmth, and
- **emotional** needs, like being loved.

▶ Look at the pictures and see if you can find some of these needs.
Copy and complete this table:

Physical needs	Emotional needs
warmth	being loved

▶ Discuss in groups what you think the following need from their parents:
- a baby
- a 6-year-old
- you.

Breast feeding

During Ruth's pregnancy, she decided to breast feed her baby after its birth.
She found out lots of information about the advantages of natural breast milk (produced by mammary glands) over the formula milk used in bottle feeding.
Breast milk contains all the nutrients a baby needs, as well as **antibodies** that fight infections.

---

1 Copy and complete:
The baby is ready to be born after . . . . weeks. Normally it is lying . . . . downwards inside the . . . . of the mother. It . . . . out through the mother's . . . . It moves because of . . . . of the wall of the uterus.

2 How do you think Jim could have helped Ruth during the birth of their baby?

3 Mothers take their babies to the clinic for check-ups (post-natal care). What sort of things do you think the nurse would check?

4 Look at the table below.
a) Draw a bar-chart to show the time between fertilisation and birth in the animals listed.
b) Can you see any pattern?

Animal	Time between fertilisation and birth (months)
hamster	0.5
rabbit	1
cat	2
sheep	5
chimpanzee	7
human	9
horse	11
elephant	20

Things to do

Adolescence

Learn about:
● changes that take place in adolescence
● the menstrual cycle

As babies grow into children, and children become teenagers, cells in the body divide and increase in size.

Adolescence is a time of change in our lives. During this time each of us changes from a child into a young adult. Our bodies change and so do our emotions.

▶ Have you found a photograph of you when you were 8 or 9 years old? Swap your photograph with that of your friend.

How do you think your friend has changed?

How do you think you've changed?

Puberty is the first stage of adolescence. Most changes in our bodies occur at this time. Not everybody starts puberty at the same time. Girls usually start before boys.

▶ Look at some of the pupils in Years 8 and 9 of your school. Can you see that many of the girls are taller than many of the boys?

If you look at those in Year 11 what do you see? Many of the boys will have caught up with and overtaken the girls.

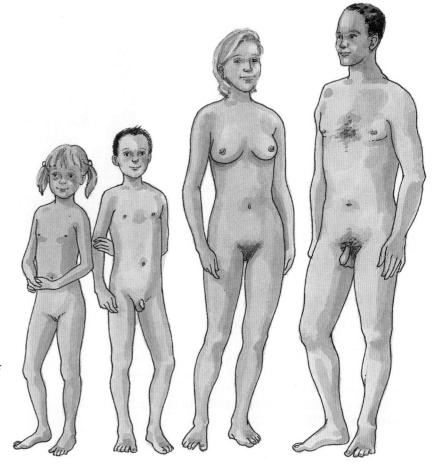

▶ Look at this picture of 9-year-old children and their parents.

a Write down the changes that have taken place between the boy and the man.

b Write down the changes that have taken place between the girl and the woman.

There are some other changes that occur that you can't see in the picture. The table opposite lists some of these changes:

What do you think causes all of these changes?

In a word the answer is '**hormones**'. Hormones are chemicals made in our bodies. Female sex hormones are made by the ovaries. Male sex hormones are made by the testes.

Girls	Boys
ovaries start to release eggs	testes start to make sperms
monthly periods begin	voice becomes deeper ('breaks')

It's a fact!

Many teenagers get spots or acne. This is not due to dirtiness. It's caused by sex hormones and disappears once adolescence is over.

Periods

One change that happens to girls during puberty is they start having periods. So what do we mean by a period?

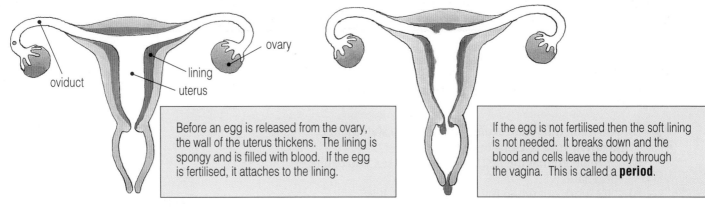

Before an egg is released from the ovary, the wall of the uterus thickens. The lining is spongy and is filled with blood. If the egg is fertilised, it attaches to the lining.

If the egg is not fertilised then the soft lining is not needed. It breaks down and the blood and cells leave the body through the vagina. This is called a **period**.

A girl's period lasts about 3 to 7 days. Periods usually occur once every 28–31 days, but this can vary. At first periods may be irregular, but as a girl gets older her periods become more regular. Girls can choose sanitary towels or tampons to absorb the flow of blood.

c What do you think would happen to the lining of the uterus if the egg was fertilised?

Emotions

During adolescence our feelings also start to change.
Suddenly we find the opposite sex more interesting and attractive.
Girls and boys start to look at themselves and ask questions such as:
Am I normal?
Am I too tall or too fat?
Am I attractive to the opposite sex?

▶ In groups, discuss some 'problem letters' written by teenagers.

Do you think the writers are right to be worried?

Write a reply to one of them.

---

1 Copy this diagram and use it to answer the following questions.

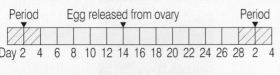

a) How often does a period occur?
b) How long does a period last?
c) On which day is an egg released?
d) Mark on your diagram the time when fertilisation is most likely to occur.

2 Why do you think the thick lining of the uterus is needed?

3 An egg is released from a girl's ovary on April 2nd. When will the next egg probably be released:
- April 30th
- May 8th or
- April 14th?

4 Why won't a woman have a period when she is pregnant?

Things to do

Questions

1　a) What happens to human sperms after they are released into the woman's body?

　　b) What happens to a human egg after it has been fertilised?

2　Do you think that there is any truth in these statements? Write down your reasons in each case.

　　a) "I've heard that the first time you have sex you can't get pregnant."

　　b) "If I work out when my egg is released, it is perfectly safe to have sex at other times."

3　Look at this diagram of twin babies inside the uterus:

　　a) Write down the letters A to D and give the name of each part.

　　b) What do you think happens to each of these parts during birth?

　　c) The twin on the right side of the diagram is better placed for birth than the twin on the left. In what way?

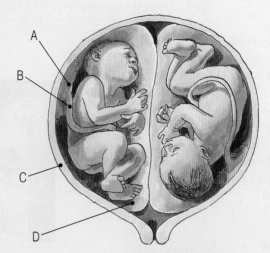

4　How do you think a father can be helpful:

　　a) during the mother's pregnancy?

　　b) during the birth?

5　a) Make a list of 4 ways in which a girl's body changes during puberty.

　　b) Make a list of 4 ways in which a boy's body changes during puberty.

6　Karen is 14. She says:

"I seem to fall out with my parents all the time these days. We argue about where I go, the friends I'm with, even the clothes I wear! We used to get on so well together. Is it my fault? What's happening to me?"

What advice can you give Karen?

7　Mark and Sharon are both 16. They have been going steady for two years. Its Friday night and Sharon has had to go away for the weekend with her parents to a wedding. Mark has nothing to do. His mates call round for him and persuade him to go to the local club disco.

At the disco, Mark notices Joanne. His mates say Joanne has always fancied him …

Write 2 different endings to the story. In one, show that Mark has a caring, responsible attitude towards Sharon. In the other, show that he hasn't.

7C

What is your environment?

It includes your house, your school, your street – in fact, all of your surroundings.

Animals and plants are affected by their environment.

This unit is about how living things depend upon their environment for their survival.

sparrowhawk

caterpillar

butterfly

oak leaves

squirrel

jay

robin

badger

acorn

mushrooms

grass snake

stoat

lichen

grass

frog

fly

toad

primrose

slug

bank vole

blackberries

foxglove

A place to live

Learn about:
- differences between habitats
- adaptations to habitats
- sampling animals from different habitats

The place in which a plant or animal lives is called its **habitat**. The **habitat** must provide everything that the living thing needs to survive.

▶ Your house is part of your habitat. What does it provide for you?

▶ Make a list of some things that animals need to survive. Make a list of some things that plants need to survive.

▶ Look at the photographs and write down how each living thing is able to survive in its own habitat.

Cactus plants live in dry habitats. Their leaves are sharp spines. They store water inside their thick stems.

Water boatmen live in ponds. They often swim to the surface of the water.

Many woodland birds build their nests in holes in trees.

Angler fish live in the deep sea. No plants live there as it is always dark.

How do small animals survive?

Small animals live in habitats around your school. Because they live there successfully we say that they are **adapted** to the habitat. They will not be easy to see. Many small creatures hide in long grass, under leaves and in cracks in bark or rocks. Many come out only at night. Here are some ways of finding animals. Choose the one that best suits the habitat.

Pooters

These are small containers with two tubes attached. You suck in through one tube and point the other at the small animal you want to collect. The gauze makes sure you don't get a mouthful of insect. Make sure you suck through the right tube!

My goodness! It's windy today!

Sweep nets

Many insects hide in long grass. A strong net is swept through the grass about 10 times so that the insects drop off into the net bag. You can use a pooter to collect them from the bag.

Uh-uh!

Tree beating

Trees and bushes provide food for many small animals. You can collect them by placing a white sheet under a branch. Shake or bang the branch with a stick so that the animals fall out. Take care not to damage the branch. Collect the animals with a pooter.

Pitfall traps

You can set yoghurt pots into holes in the ground. The rim of the pot must be level with the soil surface.

Look at the picture. How do you think small animals get trapped?

Don't sink the rim below soil level or water may enter. Pitfall traps should be left overnight.

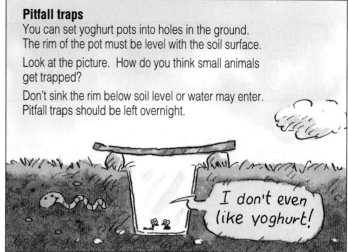

I don't even like yoghurt!

▶ Use a hand lens to study the animals that you have collected.
Be very careful not to damage them.
Your teacher will give you a sheet to help you find out their names.

▶ Where exactly are they found? Do they live on particular food plants? Are they well camouflaged? If so why? What conditions do they like to live in? Do they prefer light or dark? Dry or damp?

▶ Record your findings in a table like this:

Name of animal	Number in sample	How is it adapted to living in its habitat?
Centipede	2	Moves very fast on many legs. Has large jaws.

Return all animals, unharmed, to where you found them.

▶ Plan an enquiry to monitor environmental changes in a habitat over a period of 24 hours. Find out the range of data-logging equipment you have available.

▶ Find out which animals are active in daylight and which are active at night-time in the habitat chosen.

Things to do

1 Match up the following living things with their correct habitats:

moss	pond
trout	hedge
squirrel	path
frog	stream
dandelion	wall
hawthorn	wood

2 List some conditions that make life difficult in the following habitats:
a) stream   c) seashore rock-pool
b) hedge   d) mountain.

3 Explorers have been able to survive in very bad conditions. How have they stayed alive:
a) in outer space?
b) at the bottom of the sea?
c) in the frozen Arctic?

4 Write a letter to your pen friend on the planet Zorgan. Explain what conditions are like on Earth. Talk about your own habitat and the animals and plants that share it with you.

7C2

Changing seasons

Learn about:
● adaptations to seasonal change
● adaptations to extreme environments

We notice the weather getting colder in the winter and we put on warmer clothes. But how do animals and plants survive the changes?

▶ Look at these 4 photographs. Discuss with the others in your group which photograph was taken in which season. Give reasons for your choice.

Plants in winter

A garden in winter looks very bare compared with in summer. Many plants seem to have disappeared. Many of those that you can see have lost all their leaves. Why do you think this is?

Many plants survive the winter as seeds in the ground. What happens to these in the next spring or summer?

▶ Look at this picture of a daffodil. How do you think it is able to stay alive below the ground in winter?

Many trees lose their leaves in order to survive in winter. They grow new leaves in the spring.

▶ List 3 trees that lose their leaves in winter.
List 3 trees or shrubs that keep their leaves all year round.
Look at some of these leaves. Write down your ideas about why they're good leaves for winter.

A

B

C

D

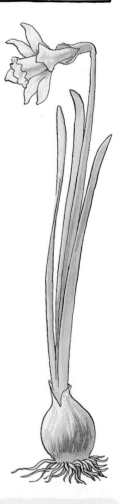

Shivering seeds!

Gardeners usually sow pea seeds at the end of the spring.
They do this so that the young pea plants are not killed by frost.
The plants grow and the new peas can be picked in the summer.

Some new varieties of pea seeds are able to survive frost.
This means that they can be sown earlier in the year.
Why would this be useful to the gardener?

Plan an investigation to find out how well seeds survive frost.

Remember that you must make it a fair test.

What other conditions might affect the growth of the seeds?

How long will your investigation take?

Think how you are going to record your results.

Show your plan to your teacher.

Then start your investigation.

Hibernation

Do you know where all the greenfly go in winter? They lay eggs with a very tough coat to help them to survive the cold. The old greenfly then die and the new greenfly hatch out in the spring.

Ladybirds feed on greenfly, but in the winter they have no food. So ladybirds **hibernate** in cracks in bark and under dead leaves.

Many small animals like hedgehogs, squirrels, dormice and frogs hibernate. They eat a lot towards the end of the summer and build up a layer of fat under their skin. Then they find a quiet spot and go to sleep for the winter.

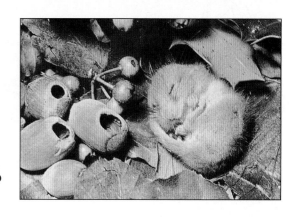

▶ Write down your answers to these questions.

a Give some reasons why animals hibernate.

b How are they able to go without food for so long?

c What do you think will happen to the fat layer during the winter?

Migration

Have you seen birds flying off in the autumn? Swallows and martins escape the winter by flying to warmer countries. This is called **migration**.

▶ List some of the problems that birds face in winter.

Some birds visit Britain in the winter. Birds like Bewick's swans and pink-footed geese arrive in this country in the autumn. They come from the colder north and escape even harsher conditions found there.

▶ Look at the map showing the migration routes of 4 birds.

d Which two birds do you think are summer visitors to Britain?

e Which do you think are winter visitors to Britain?

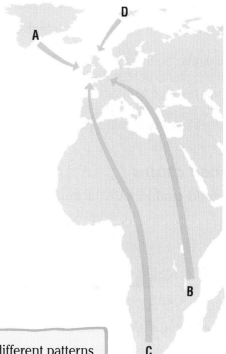

---

1 How do each of the following pass the winter:
a) hedgehog?
b) swallow?
c) greenfly?
d) Bewick's swan?

2 Some animals undergo changes in order to survive the winter.
a) Some animals like the stoat and birds like the ptarmigan have white coats in winter. Why do you think this is?
b) Many wild animals grow thick coats in winter. So do cats and dogs. Why do you think this is?

3 Discuss how you could help garden birds to survive the winter. Make a poster to encourage others to care for birds in winter.

4 Different climates have different patterns of rainfall throughout the year.
a) Plot 2 graphs using the following sets of rainfall data.

Month	Rainfall in mm	
Jan	55	60
Feb	50	80
Mar	30	170
Apr	20	250
May	15	23
June	5	120
July	0	80
Aug	0	80
Sept	20	90
Oct	20	90
Nov	50	140
Dec	60	130

b) Study the rainfall patterns shown and label your graphs with either Entebbe (tropical forest) or Alice Springs (hot desert).

Things to do

Who's eating who?

Learn about:
● energy transfers in food chains
● linking food chains to form food webs

Why do you think cows, horses and sheep spend so much time eating? They eat mainly grass.
Animals that eat plants are called **herbivores**.

▶ Make a list of some other herbivores.

Animals such as lions, owls and foxes feed on meat.
We call animals that eat other animals **carnivores**.

▶ Make a list of some other carnivores.

How do you think plants feed?
Green plants get their energy from the Sun.
They are able to change light energy into chemical energy in food.
They are the only living things able to do this.
Green plants are called **producers**.

Food chains

A **food chain** shows the ***movement of energy*** between plants and animals.

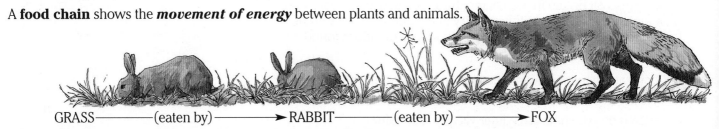

GRASS————(eaten by)————▶RABBIT————(eaten by)————▶FOX

The arrows shows the direction in which the energy flows from one to another.

Here is a food chain with 4 organisms:

GRASS————▶GRASSHOPPER————▶FIELDMOUSE————▶OWL

Notice that the food chain always begins with a producer (green plant).
This can include parts of a plant such as buds or fruits or even dead leaves.
Some animals feed only upon dead plants and animals.

DEAD LEAVES————▶WOODLOUSE————▶BLACKBIRD

You are also part of some food chains. Think of some of the things that you eat. Here is one example of a food chain that might involve you:

GRASS————▶SHEEP————▶HUMAN

▶ Write down some other food chains that include you.
Use arrows to show which way the energy is going.

▶ Look at the woodland picture at the beginning of this topic (page 35).
See how many food chains you can find. Write them down.
Use arrows to show the direction of the energy flow.

Looking at animals in leaf litter

Put some leaf litter into a white tray.

Carefully sort through it and collect any small animals that you find. You can pick them up with a fine paint brush or by using a pooter.

Be careful that you don't damage them.

Your teacher will give you a sheet showing what each animal eats.
Try to write down possible food chains for the leaf litter and include larger animals.
Look for any signs of feeding by larger animals near the place you collected your leaf litter.
What clues can you search for?
Wash your hands after this activity.

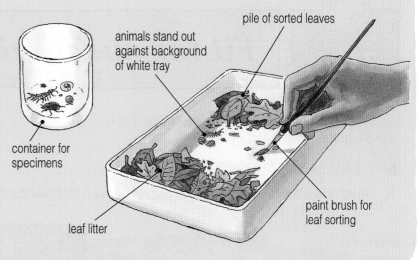

Food webs

Most animals will eat more than one thing. Frogs would get pretty fed up if they just ate slugs. They also eat snails and different types of insects.

A **food web** is made up of many food chains. It gives a more complete picture of how animals feed.

▶ Look at this woodland food web. Try to find all the food chains and write them down. There are 6 for you to look for.

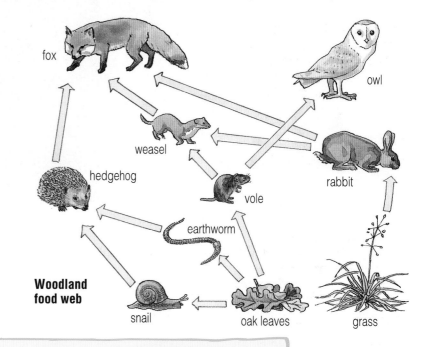

Woodland food web

1 Look back at the woodland food web.
a) Name 2 carnivores from this web.
b) Name 2 herbivores from this web.
c) Name 2 producers from this web.
d) If all the foxes died, what do you think would happen to the number of:
   i) hedgehogs? ii) snails?

2 Why does a food chain always begin with a green plant?

3 Look at these 2 food chains:

GRAIN → CHICKEN → HUMAN

GRAIN → HUMAN

Which of these food chains provides most food for people?
Why do you think this is?

4 Look at this seashore food web.

Seashore food web

a) What do dog whelks feed on?
b) If the dog whelks were all killed by pollution, what would happen to the number of: i) flatfish? ii) barnacles?
c) Draw a food chain with 5 organisms from this food web.
d) How many carnivores are there in this food web?

Things to do

Fit for survival

Learn about:
- adaptations to habitats
- plannning a biological enquiry

Animals and plants have things about them that help them to survive in the place that they live.

▶ Look at the photographs.

Write down the things about each animal or plant that you think helps them to survive.

Oxford ragwort

polar bear

flounder

mole

eyed hawk moth

The animals and plants in the photographs are **adapted** to living in particular habitats.
They have special **adaptations** that help them to survive.

▶ List some of the adaptations that help *you* to survive.

Survival is the name of the game

Here are 2 animals that are adapted to live in harsh environments.

▶ List the adaptations that you think each animal shows.
Then write down how each adaptation helps it to survive.

Mayfly larva

The mayfly larva lives in fast-flowing streams.

It clings tightly underneath rocks.

It has a flattened body with a very streamlined shape.

It feeds upon small plants growing on the rocks.

It has **gills** along the sides of its body and eyes on the top of its head.

It always moves away from the light into cracks between the stones.

Limpet

The limpet lives on the seashore.

It uses a sucker to cling tightly to rocks when the tide is out.

It has a thick shell to protect it from very high and very low temperatures.

It feeds on young seaweeds and it breathes using a gill to take in oxygen from the water.

Lice are nice!

Look carefully at your woodlice with a hand-lens.
Be careful not to damage them in any way.
How do you think they are adapted for living in leaf litter**?**

What conditions do you think woodlice like**?**
Make a list of your ideas (hypotheses).
You can use a **choice chamber** to find out if your ideas are right.

Plan an investigation to find out what conditions woodlice like.
Remember to make it a fair test.

- How many woodlice will you use? Why**?**
- How will you record your results**?**

Show your plan to your teacher, then try it out.

Choice chamber

---

1 How do you think that each of the following helps the animals to survive?
a) Deer and antelope are usually found together in herds.
b) Hoverflies have yellow stripes and look like wasps. But they are flies and have no sting.
c) Ragworms have good reflexes and can move back quickly into their burrows.

2 Suggest ways in which you think humans have been able to survive in the following environments:
a) hot desert
b) polar regions
c) highly populated cities.

3 Look at the numbers of eggs laid by these animals:

	Number of eggs
cod	3 million
frog	1000
snake	12
thrush	5

a) Why do you think the fish lays so many eggs?
b) Why does the snake lay far fewer eggs than the frog?
c) Why does a thrush lay so few eggs?

4 Look at these different bird beaks. Write down the name of each bird and say how you think its beak adapts it for survival.

Things to do

golden eagle

woodpecker

woodcock   wigeon

Life and death

Learn about:
- adaptations of predators and prey
- changes in the structure of food webs

Predators are animals that kill other animals for food.

The animals that they kill are called **prey**.

▶ Make a list of 5 animals that you think are predators.

a Predators are usually bigger and fewer in number than their prey. Why do you think this is**?**

Look at the tiger:
It seems to have some unbeatable weapons.

▶ Think about the things that make it a good predator. Make a list.

Sometimes we think that predators have an easy time killing defenceless prey.
In fact the tiger has to work hard for its meal.
For every wild prey that it kills, the tiger fails 20–30 times.

b Predators often attack prey that is young, old, sick, weak or injured. Why do you think this is**?**

Tiger numbers have been threatened by hunting and by the destruction of their habitat.
A programme of **conservation** has given them more protection and their numbers are slowly increasing.

A tiger is a predator

The predator strikes!

Choose one person to be the 'predator' in your group and blindfold him or her.

Arrange 9 discs at random on the squared paper.

Think of each disc as a prey animal.

Now the predator must search for the discs by tapping over the paper with one finger for one minute.

Each disc that the predator touches is removed. It counts as a 'kill'.

After each 'kill', the predator must pause and count to 3 before continuing.

After one minute count the total number of 'kills'.

Repeat the experiment, increasing the number of discs each time. Try 16, 25, 50 and 100 discs.

Record your results in a table.

Draw a graph of **number of kills** against **total number of prey**.

What are your conclusions from this activity**?**

Don't get caught!

▶ Look at the hare:

c How is it adapted to escape predators?

Here are some things that help prey to survive.

Explain how each one increases the chances of their survival.

d Run, swim or fly fast.

e Stay together in large numbers.

f Taste horrible.

g Have warning colours.

Life's ups and downs

The graph shows the number of lynx (predators) and the number of hares (prey) over a number of years.

Look at the graph carefully.

If the hares have plenty of food they breed and they increase in number (see ❶).

This makes more food for the lynx, so their numbers increase (see ❷).

▶ Answer these questions about what happens next:

h Why do the numbers of hares fall at ❸?

i Why do the numbers of lynx fall at ❹?

J Why do the numbers of hares increase at ❺?

k Why are the numbers of prey usually greater than the numbers of predators?

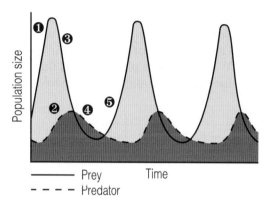

——— Prey   Time
– – – – Predator

A lynx hunts
its prey

1 What do you think makes a good predator?
Make a picture of a make-believe predator that would catch lots of prey.

2 Some people think that predators are 'bad', but humans are the greatest predators that the world has known.
Write about some ways in which humans are predators.

3 Write about ways in which each of the following are successful predators:
a) domestic cat   b) spider   c) eagle.

4 The World Wildlife Fund started 'Operation Tiger'. This was a conservation programme aimed at protecting the tiger from extinction.
What do you think they did to protect the tigers? Use secondary sources of information (books, ROMs and/or the internet).

Things to do

Questions

1 Choose: a) an insect b) a bird and c) a mammal.
For each of your choices, say where it lives (its habitat), what it
feeds on and how it is adapted to its habitat.

2 See if you can make a food chain out of these:
a) thrush, cabbage, caterpillar
b) slug, hedgehog, lettuce
c) tiny plants, fish, water fleas, tadpoles
d) greenfly, blackbird, ladybird, rose bush.

3 Look at the 3 temperature graphs below.
a) See if you can match them up with London, Singapore and Alaska.
b) Give a reason for your choice in each case.
c) Which of these places do you think would be the most difficult
for plants and animals to survive in? Give your reasons.

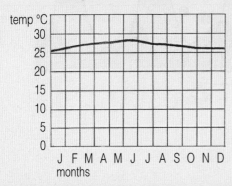

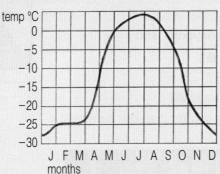

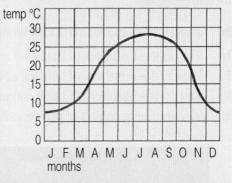

4 Look at these samples of earthworm populations taken from 15 cm
under the soil:

Month	Jan.	Feb.	Mar.	Apr.	May	Jun.	Jul.	Aug.	Sep.	Oct.	Nov.	Dec.
number of worms	12	5	7	37	45	11	5	13	36	47	98	50
temperature (°C)	2	1	1	4	7	16	19	16	13	10	7	5
rainfall (mm)	40	30	25	50	80	20	5	25	40	50	80	70

a) Under what conditions do earthworms grow most successfully?
b) What do you think happens to the earthworms in hot weather?
c) Why do you think the earthworm numbers increase in the autumn?

5 Some pupils did a survey of a small woodland
habitat. They identified and counted all the
trees. The table shows their results.
a) Draw a bar-chart of these results.
b) Which were the 2 most common trees
in the wood?

Name of tree	Number in wood
ash	8
beech	15
birch	20
holly	2
oak	4

Variation and Classification

Have you ever been to the seashore?
It's an interesting and exciting place to visit.

Many creatures live there, especially in rock-pools.
Rock-pools are left behind when the tide goes out.
Each is like a small aquarium. Many plants and animals
survive in rock-pools until the tide returns.

Next time you go to the seashore, have a look to see how
many animals and plants you can find.
But be sure not to damage them. Leave them
undisturbed so that other people can look at them.

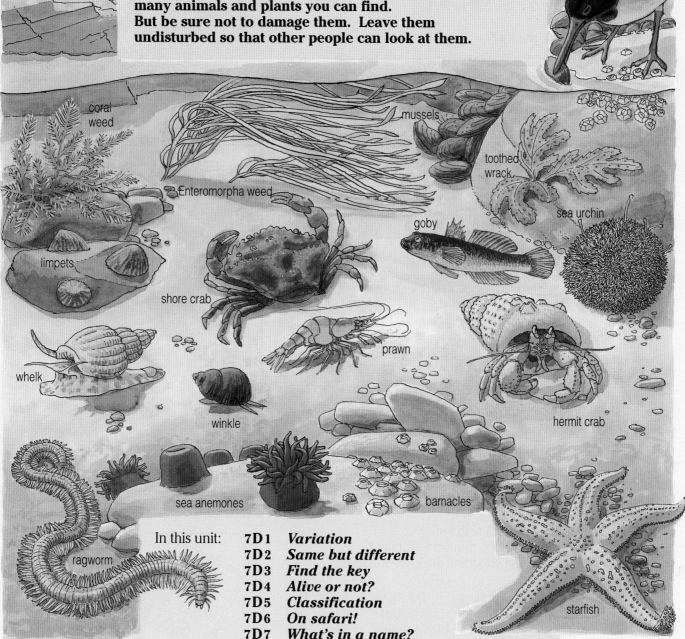

oyster catcher

coral weed

mussels

toothed wrack

Enteromorpha weed

sea urchin

goby

limpets

shore crab

prawn

hermit crab

whelk

winkle

ragworm

sea anemones

barnacles

starfish

In this unit:

7D1 *Variation*

Learn about:
- differences in individuals of a species
- using a spreadsheet to store data
- inherited and environmental characteristics

Look at the kittens in the picture:
They are all from the same litter.

a In what ways do you think they look alike?

b In what ways do you think they look different?

▶ Look around at the people in your class.
   They have a lot in common: they are all human for a start!
   But they also have features that are different.
   Make a list of some of these differences.

Why do we look like we do?

We get some of our features from our parents. We **inherit** them.
Other features do not come from our parents.
These features are caused by the way we lead our life.
We call these features **environmental**.

Can you roll your tongue like the girl in the photograph?

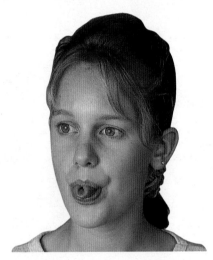

You can't learn how to do it. You have either inherited it from your
parents or you haven't.

The soccer player in the photograph has a lot of natural ability.
Do you think that this is inherited or environmental?
But to be a top-class player, strength, agility and stamina are needed.
Do you think that these are inherited or environmental?

▶ Copy out the following list of features.
   Write (i) after those that you think are inherited,
   and   (e) after those that you think are environmental.

shape of nose	neat writing	freckles	hair colour
hair length	scars	skill at languages	an accent
eye colour	good at sport	blood group	size of feet

How do you measure up?

Nobody's the same, we are all unique!
Collect the following information about yourself and others in your class:

> eye colour   height   left-handed *or* right-handed   shoe size
>
> length of index finger   hair colour   tongue rolling   ear lobes

Record your findings in a spreadsheet.
Some things vary **gradually**.

c   Print a bar-chart to show the number of people in your class with different length index fingers. What do you find**?**

Other things are more **clear-cut**. For instance there are only a few different types of eye colour.

d   Print a bar-chart to show the number of people in your class with different colour eyes. What do you find**?**

e   Investigate any links (correlation) between the different sets of data in your spreadsheet.

f   Evaluate the strength of any links you find.

▶   Look at the graph of the height of some pupils:

g   How many children are less than 160 cm**?**

h   What is the most common height**?**

i   Do you think that the variation shown on the graph is gradual or clear-cut**?**

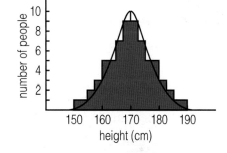

▶   Look at the graph of the hair colour of some pupils:

j   What is the most common hair colour in the class**?**

k   How is this graph different from the graph for height**?**

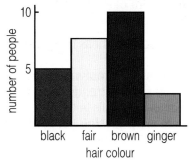

1   Copy and complete:
We . . . . many features from our parents.
Other things, like being able to ride a bike, we . . . . during our lifetime. We say that they are due to the . . . .
Some variation, like height, is . . . . Other variation, such as eye colour, is . . . .

2   Libby has just come home from 2 weeks in Majorca.
Do you think her sun-tan is inherited?
Explain your answer.

3   Mike says "I think red hair and being good at sport are both inherited."
Do you agree or disagree? Give your reasons.

4   Look at the picture of a litter of puppies:
a)   What features have the puppies inherited from their mother?
b)   What features have the puppies inherited from their father?

Things to do

49

Same but different

Learn about:
- inherited characteristics
- environmental differences
- variation in offspring

Can you remember what are the causes of variation?

You should know that variation is caused by:

- the features that we inherit,
- the features that result from our environment.

▶ Look at this family photograph:

Make a list of the features that you think the children have inherited from their parents.

Then make a list of the features that you think have been affected by the children's environment.

A snail's tale

The photograph shows some common banded snails:

a Write down some ways in which you think the snails are different.

Most of the differences will be things that you can see easily. But what about things like length of shell? You would have to measure these to find differences.

▶ Look at the top graph opposite: It shows the width of snail shell plotted against the length of snail shell.

b Do snails with longer shells have wider shells?

A 'line of best fit' has been drawn through the plotted points. This is to help you see any trends in the data. You can see that as the shells get longer, they also get wider. We say that there is a **positive correlation** between the two.

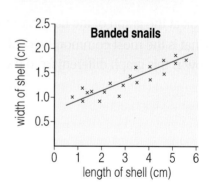

A prickly problem

Class 7GMW wanted to know if there was any connection between the length of holly leaves and the number of prickles they have. Each group collected 20 holly leaves. They measured the length and the number of prickles on each leaf.

Here is the data collected by Gemma, Mustafa and George:

c Was there a positive correlation between leaf length and number of prickles?

d Why did the group choose a sample size of 20 rather than 5?

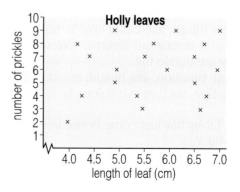

Here comes the Sun

Carry out *one* of these two investigations:

1. Do the upper leaves on a bush differ in size from the lower leaves?

2. Does the size of leaves from plants grown in sunny habitats differ from the size of leaves of plants grown in shady habitats?

Whichever investigation you choose to carry out, make a plan. Think about:

- Choosing a large enough sample size.

- How you can safely collect your samples.

- How you will work out the size of each leaf. (Hint: you could draw around the leaf on graph paper and then count the number of squares.)

- What sort of graphs you will draw. Can you enter your data on a spreadsheet?

- What conclusions you can draw from your analysis. Is there any correlation in your data?

Comment on the strength of your evidence.

Produce a full report of your investigation.

Dog's mercury growing in shade   Dog's mercury growing in sun

---

Things to do

1 Copy and complete:
Children in the same family are usually . . . ., but they can show . . . . This variation may be due to the information that they have . . . . from their parents. The variation could also be due to the effects of their . . . . Identical twins would not weigh the same if they were fed on different . . . . or if they carried out different amounts of . . . .

2 The data shows the heights of two groups of boys in centimetres. Group A were born in 1900 and group B in 1960.

Group	Age									
	7	8	9	10	11	12	13	14	15	16
A	108	112	116	120	124	128	131	138	144	150
B	115	123	127	130	137	140	148	155	160	165

a) Plot the data in the best way you can.
b) Are the differences in height inherited or environmental?
c) Explain your answer to part b).

3 Carry out an investigation to see whether or not there is any correlation between the height and hand span of pupils in your year-group.
a) What sample size will you use?
b) Will you choose boys or girls?
c) How will you collect your results?
d) How will you display your results?
e) How will your analysis show if there is any correlation?

4 Look at the tree in the photograph:
a) Is its shape due to inherited or environmental causes?
b) Explain how you came to your conclusion.

Find the key

Learn about:
- comparing living things by observation
- using keys to identify living things

Scientists use **keys** to identify living things.
They use these to **classify** living things into groups.
A key has a number of questions.
You start at the beginning and answer "yes" or "no" to each question.
It will soon take you to the animal or plant you want.

▶ Use this key to identify these birds:

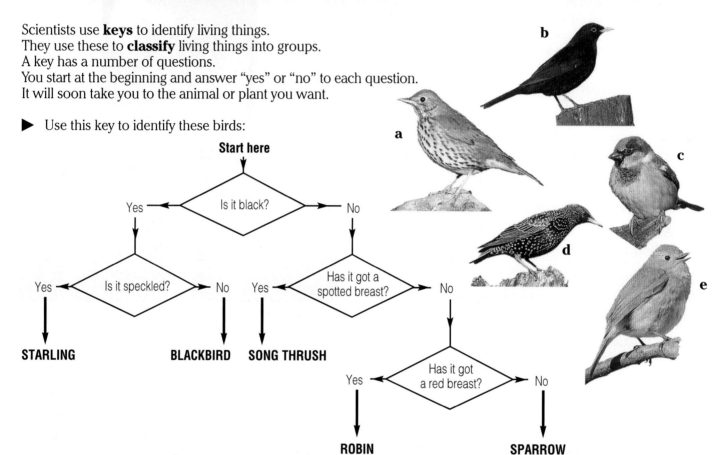

Start here

Is it black? — Yes / No

Yes → Is it speckled? → No

Has it got a spotted breast? — Yes / No

STARLING   **BLACKBIRD**   **SONG THRUSH**

Has it got a red breast? — Yes / No

ROBIN   **SPARROW**

Use the next key to identify 5 small animals found in grassland.
It is set out differently from the first key, but works in the same way.
Start at the beginning and answer the question at each stage.

1	Has legs	Go to 2
	Has no legs	Snail
2	Has 3 or 4 pairs of legs	Go to 3
	Has more than 3 or 4 pairs of legs	Centipede
3	Has 3 pairs of legs	Go to 4
	Has 4 pairs of legs	Spider
4	Has spots on body	Ladybird
	Has no spots on body	Ground beetle

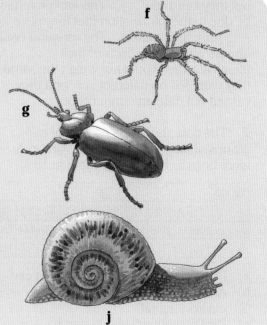

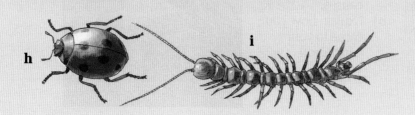

Leaf it out!

Now try making a key of your own.

1 Put the 6 leaves out in front of you.
2 Think of a question that divides them into 2 groups.
   Write the question down.
3 Now think up questions to divide each group into two.
   Write these down.
4 Carry on until you come to each leaf.
5 Write your key out neatly and then try it out on a friend.

▶ Now try making a key of these pond animals.
  Do they have legs or not? What are their body shapes like?
  Remember to split them up using one question at a time.

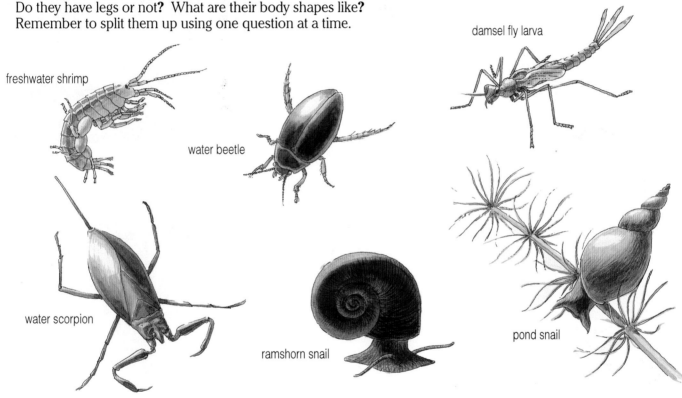

freshwater shrimp

water beetle

damsel fly larva

water scorpion

ramshorn snail

pond snail

Keys are good fun and get easier to use with practice.
Your teacher can give you more keys to try out.

Things to do

1 We can classify plants and animals into groups. Research and write down:
a) the 4 main groups that make up the plant kingdom
b) the 5 main vertebrate groups (see page 59)
c) any 6 groups of invertebrates (see page 56).

2 Write down the features that would enable you to classify a fish, an amphibian, a reptile, a bird and a mammal (see page 59).
Now make a key that you could use to identify each of these vertebrate groups.

3 Research and write down some features of each of the 4 main groups of plants.
Make a key, using these features, that you could use to identify each group of plants.

4 In the 18th century, Carl Linnaeus worked out a way of naming all living things.
He gave them 2 names (called a **genus** and a **species**). His name for you is *Homo sapiens*.
Find out what you can about Carl Linnaeus using ROMs, the internet and books.

Alive or not?

Learn about:
- living and non-living things
- plants and animals are the main groups of living things

How can you tell if something is alive or not?

▶ Write down as many ideas as you can about what *all* living things do.
Discuss whether your ideas are true for each of the following:
- rabbit
- table
- tree
- robot
- cheese

▶ The table below shows some more ideas about being alive.
The non-living thing in the table is a car engine.
The living thing can be an animal of your choice.
It could be you!

Draw the table and answer the questions.
The first one is done for you.

	Animal (living)	Car engine (non-living)
Does it need air?	yes	yes
Does it move?		
Can it grow?		
Does it need food (fuel)?		
Can it feed on its own?		
Does it give out waste?		
Can it feel things?		
Will it die when it is old?		
Can it be a parent?		
Can it be eaten by another living thing?		

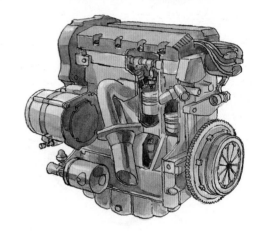

Energy matters

Living things need energy to stay alive.
Can you remember where living things get their energy from?

Sugar is a food that gives us a lot of energy.
Sugar is broken down inside animals and plants to get the energy out
We call this **respiration**.

SUGAR + OXYGEN = CARBON DIOXIDE + WATER + ENERGY FOR LIFE

Oxygen is needed for respiration to take place.
When sugar burns in oxygen it releases energy.
What else do you think is produced?

Explorations Unlimited

Dear Scientists,

One of our expeditions has found something interesting in Death Valley. They are not sure, but they may have found some very rare seeds. We want to know whether they are alive or not?

Please plan and carry out an investigation to find out if the seeds are living or not. Remember to make it a fair test and send me your report.

Thanks Des Covery

Plants: the green machines

Do you know what plants can do that most other living things can't?

They can make their own food by a process called **photosynthesis**. In their leaves they have a green substance called **chlorophyll**. With this they can use energy from sunlight to make sugars.

Differences between plants and animals

The 2 main groups of living things are plants and animals

▶ Copy and complete this table to show the main differences between these 2 groups of living things.

Plants	Animals
1. Don't move around much	1. Move around a lot
2.	2.

Things to do

1 There are some robots that can move and that are sensitive to such things as smells and sounds.
Why do we say they are not alive?

2 Do you know of any plants that provide food for humans as a result of photosynthesis? Make a list and say which part of the plant you think is eaten, e.g. root, leaf, seed, etc.

3 Copy out the activities listed in the left-hand column, then match each with the correct example from the right-hand column:

GROWING	escaping from danger
RESPIRING	becoming a parent
GETTING RID OF WASTE	increasing your body size
MOVING	smelling food
REPRODUCING	having a snack
FEEDING	going to the loo
USING SENSES	using up energy in a race

Classification

Learn about:
- the importance of classification
- the major groups of invertebrates and vertebrates

There are millions of different kinds of plants and animals in the world.

▶ Make a list of 10 animals by yourself.

Compare your list with others in your group.

Each different kind of plant and animal is called a **species**. You have listed 10 species of animal.

Over the years scientists have tried to give every species of plant and animal a name of its own.

▶ Why do you think this has been difficult?

It has been made easier by putting similar living things into groups
This is called **classification**.

▶ The 2 biggest groups are plants and animals. What decides whether a living thing is a plant or an animal?

To make it even easier to identify living things we break the big groups into smaller groups.

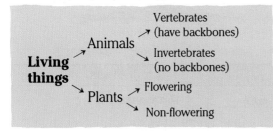

Living things
- Animals
  - Vertebrates (have backbones)
  - Invertebrates (no backbones)
- Plants
  - Flowering
  - Non-flowering

▶ Which of the groups in the diagram above do you belong to?

▶ How many vertebrates can your group name in one minute?

Invertebrates (animals without backbones)

Jellyfish and sea anemones Jelly-like body. Have tentacles with stinging cells to catch food

Flatworms Flattened body with no segments

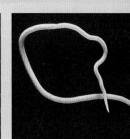

Roundworms Long thin body with no segments

Segmented worms Long, tube-shaped body made of segments

Molluscs Many have a shell. Body not in segments. Move around on a muscular foot

Starfish and sea urchin 5 'arms' or star-shaped pattern on their bodies. Spiny skins

Arthropods Jointed legs. Body has hard outer skeleton

The arthropods are a group of invertebrates wit jointed legs. They can be divided into 4 smaller groups:

Arthropods

Crustaceans ('cru-stations') Chalky outer skeleton. Most live in water

Insects 6 legs. 3 parts to the body. Have wings

Spiders 8 legs. 2 parts to the body. No wings

Centipedes and milliped Long body made up of segments. Many legs

► Look back at the picture of the rock-pool on page 47.

a There are many invertebrates in the picture. Use the information on the previous page to decide which group each belongs to.

b The goby and the oystercatcher are vertebrates. To which group do you think each belongs?

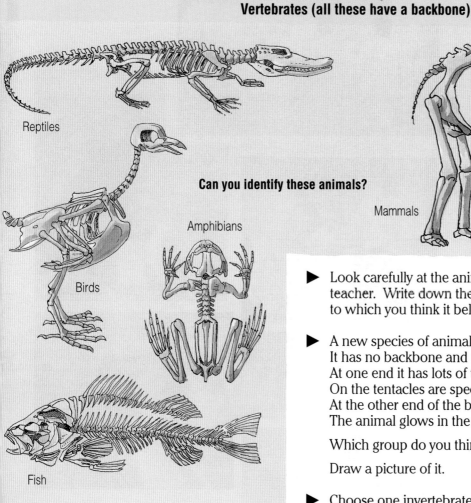

Vertebrates (all these have a backbone)

Reptiles

Can you identify these animals?

Amphibians

Birds

Fish

Mammals

► Look carefully at the animal specimens provided by your teacher. Write down the name of each animal and the group to which you think it belongs.

► A new species of animal has just been found in the deep sea. It has no backbone and no legs. At one end it has lots of tentacles around its mouth. On the tentacles are special cells that sting its prey. At the other end of the body is a sucker for sticking it to rocks. The animal glows in the dark.

Which group do you think the animal belongs to?

Draw a picture of it.

► Choose one invertebrate group. Make up an animal that could belong to the group and draw it. Get your friend to try to identify your invented animal.

1 Copy and complete:
Animals with a backbone are called . . . .
Animals that do not have a backbone are called . . . . Invertebrates with jointed legs are put into the group called . . . . This can be divided into four smaller groups called crustaceans, ... , ... and . . . . and . . . .

2 Which animal group has
a) a muscular foot?   c) 8 legs?
b) 6 legs?

3 For each of the following, choose the odd one out and try to give your reason in each case:
a) daisy, flatworm, sea urchin, butterfly
b) fly, spider, ladybird, beetle
c) snail, slug, sea anemone
d) leech, millipede, earthworm

4 Do some research to find out more about one group of invertebrates and list some examples from that group.

Things to do

On safari!

Hi, my name's Lizzie. Last Saturday I went to the Wildlife park with my friend Richard. We saw llamas with their young. It was a hot day to have such hairy coats. Next we saw a family of baboons. They were very hairy and one mother was feeding its baby. I remembered that **mammals** feed their young on milk. In a different part of the park we saw zebras and camels.

After a stop for drinks at the cafe, we walked to the **reptile** house. There were lizards and snakes from many different countries. We were able to hold the boa constrictor and we could feel its dry skin covered with scales.

We also saw some frogs, toads and salamanders. These had smooth, moist skin and a label said that they were called **amphibians**.

We went to the **bird** house next.
Here there were some very rare birds.
We saw California condors and whooping cranes.
They are in danger because the places where they live are being destroyed.
A bird of paradise had beautiful feathers.

We couldn't leave before seeing the aquarium.
There were many types of **fish** in freshwater and seawater tanks.
There were perch and roach as well as tunny, wrasse and bream.
They all had scaly skin and fins for swimming.

On the way home Richard and I talked about the animals that we had seen. Later that day I opened my science book at the page 'Vertebrates: animals with backbones'.

VERTEBRATES: ANIMALS WITH BACK BONES

MAMMALS
Have hair or fur
Feed young on milk
Give birth to live young

BIRDS
Have feathers and wings
Most can fly
Lay eggs with hard shells

REPTILES
Have dry, scaly skin
Lay eggs with soft shells

AMPHIBIANS
Have smooth, moist skin
Breed in water

FISH
Live all of the time in water
Swim using fins
Breathe using gills
Have scaly skin

▶ Copy out this table:

Mammals	Birds	Reptiles	Amphibians	Fish
Llamas				

Read through the story and write down the name of each animal mentioned in the correct column of your table.

▶ Write down 3 reasons why you think vertebrates need a skeleton.

It's a fact!

Archaeopteryx was an early type of bird living 150 million years ago. The fossil remains show that it had feathers (like birds) but also teeth (like reptiles). Draw a picture of what you think the bird looked like.

1 Copy and complete:
All vertebrates belong to one of five main groups. The . . . . live in water all the time, breathe using . . . . and swim using . . . .
The . . . . live part of their life on land but go to water to . . . . The . . . . have scaly skin and live all their life on land. . . . . are the only group of vertebrates that can fly. They have . . . . and . . . . to do this. . . . . have fur or . . . . and feed their young on . . . .

2 Which group do you think you belong to? Give your reasons.

3 Find out the names of 2 examples of each of the 5 main vertebrate groups that live wild in Britain.

4 A penguin and an osprey look very different. Write down 3 reasons why scientists think they belong to the same group.

Things to do

5 In what ways do you think reptiles are better than amphibians at living on land?

What's in a name?

Learn about:
● the worldwide naming system that helps scientists study living things

What do the ox-eye daisy, the dog daisy and marguerite have in common?
The answer is that they are all the same plant.
But they have different names in different parts of Britain.

a Why do you think that using 'common names' can be confusing?

Well if you wanted to describe a particular plant or animal to someone in another country, you would be speaking in different languages.

Luckily we have a **binomial system** of naming living things. This gives every living thing **2** names: the first name is the **genus** and the second is the **species**.

For instance, Homo sapiens is the **_scientific name_** for a human.

b What do we mean by a species?

A species is a very similar group of individuals that can breed together and produce fertile offspring.
For example, all domestic dogs belong to the same species.
They may look different, but they can mate and give birth to cross-breeds that are perfectly healthy.

Grouping species

▶ Look at the diagram, which shows how we **classify** the grizzly bear.

c What is the largest group of individuals in the diagram?

d What is the smallest grouping in the diagram called?

Can you see that we can classify living things on the basis of their **_shared_** features?

e Use the diagram to list the groups in order of size. Start with the smallest and end up with the largest group.

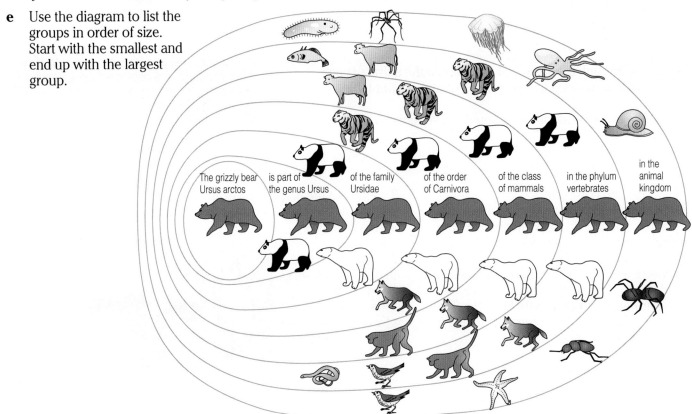

The grizzly bear Ursus arctos | is part of the genus Ursus | of the family Ursidae | of the order of Carnivora | of the class of mammals | in the phylum vertebrates | in the animal kingdom

The name game

This game will help you revise invertebrate classification.

Choose a partner and sit opposite each other.

You will both be given 16 cards each with a picture and description of an invertebrate that lives in freshwater.

Lay out your 16 cards face-up on the table in front of you.

Your partner keeps his or her cards hidden and picks out *one* card, looks at it and places it in an envelope – so you don't know which it is.

You now have to ask questions based upon the pictures and descriptions to try and find out which invertebrate is in the envelope.

But your partner is only allowed to answer 'yes' or 'no'.

Write down the question that you ask each time.

Turn over the cards that you eliminate with each question.

Eventually you will identify the invertebrate chosen by your partner.

Now swap roles and see how many questions your partner needs to ask to identify the invertebrate that you choose.

The person with the *fewest* questions wins '**The name game!**'

Things to do

1 Copy and complete:
A group of organisms that can mate and produce . . . .
offspring is called a . . . .
The study of how we put living things into groups is called . . . .
It uses the . . . . system by giving every living thing 2 names.
The first is called the . . . . name and the second the . . . . name.
We classify living things on the basis of their . . . . features.

2 The arthropods are a phylum of jointed-legged animals.
a) Can you name the 4 main classes?
b) Give an example of an animal from each of these classes.

3 The plants are classified into 4 main groups.
a) Can you name each of these groups?
b) Give an example of a plant from each group.

4 The vertebrates make up one phylum.
a) What feature do all vertebrates have?
b) Name the 5 main classes of vertebrates.
c) Give an example of an animal from each of these classes.
d) To which class of vertebrates do each of the following belong:
    i) a turtle? ii) a bat? iii) a whale?
    iv) a salamander? v) a snake?

To which class of arthropods do these belong?

Questions

1 A visitor from outer space lands on Earth.
The first thing that it sees is a steam train passing by.
Give 2 reasons why the visitor thinks it is alive.
Give 2 reasons why you think the visitor is wrong.

2 Look at this photograph of an animal:
Do you think it is vertebrate or
an invertebrate?
Which group do you think it belongs to?
Write down your reasons for your choice.

3 Who am I?
a) I have 6 legs, and wings.
b) I have smooth, damp skin and spend part of my life in water.
c) I have a shell and move around on a muscular foot.
d) I have feathers and wings. I can fly!
e) I have 8 legs but no wings.

4 a) Are these animals vertebrates or invertebrates?
b) Give a reason for your answer to part a).
c) Put each animal into its correct group based on features that
you can see.

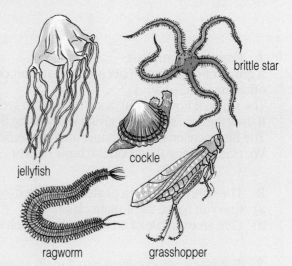

brittle star

cockle

jellyfish

ragworm   grasshopper

5 What features do you think that you have inherited from
a) your mother?   b) your father?
If you have a sister or brother, have they inherited the same
features?

6 Bob and Baz are identical twins:
What features have they inherited from their parents?
What features are the result of their environment?

7 Some pupils did a survey on the size of foxglove fruits.
Here are their results:

Length of fruit (mm)	20	21	22	23	24	25	26	27	28	29
Number collected	4	6	14	22	30	26	18	12	12	3

a) Draw a bar-chart of their results.
b) What sort of variation do you think this shows?

Acids and alkalis

7E

Have you heard of acids and alkalis?
What do you know about them already?

These substances are important to us in everyday life.
They are used to make clothes, paints, soaps, fertilisers,
medicines and many other things.

There are even acids and alkalis inside your body!
Your stomach wall makes acid. If too much acid is made,
it can be a problem. In this unit you can find out how to
solve the problem.

You might also think about the 'hydrangea plant mystery'.
How can you make the plant grow blue flowers this year …
and pink flowers next year?

Acid or alkali?

Learn about:
- common acids and alkalis
- hazard signs
- safe working with hazards

▶ Write down 5 words that come to mind when you hear the word **acid**.

▶ What do you think an acid is?
You could use some of your 5 words to help you write a sentence.
I think an acid is …

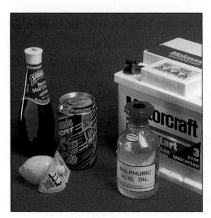

All these contain acids

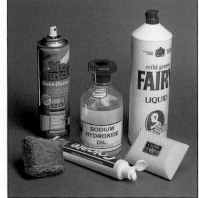

All these contain alkalis

▶ Think of as many examples as you can of scientific opposites, e.g. conductor/insulator.

Acids and **alkalis** are *chemical* opposites.

Indicators can be used to show which things are acids and which things are alkalis.

Have you ever used **litmus** indicator?
Litmus is a useful indicator. It can be in the form of a paper or a liquid. It is a purple dye which turns *red* in acid and *blue* in alkali.

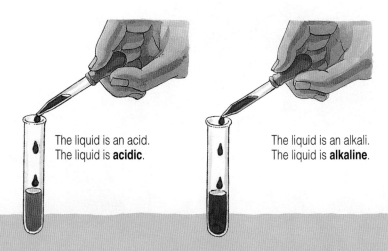

The liquid is an acid.
The liquid is **acidic**.

The liquid is an alkali.
The liquid is **alkaline**.

Making your own indicators

Some brightly coloured berries, flower petals and vegetables make good indicators.

Look at the pictures to see how you can make your own indicator.

methylated spirit

flammable

plant pieces

pestle

mortar

acid

alkali

Crush your plant pieces.

Add a little methylated spirit.

Keep crushing until all the colour has come out.

Use a pipette to put some of the coloured liquid into a test-tube of dilute acid and a test-tube of dilute alkali.

Some everyday acids and alkalis are not hazardous.

Look at the photos on the previous page.
Which substances are hazardous and which are not?

A hazardous acid or alkali should have a hazard sign
displayed on its container.
Look at the hazard signs below:

Concentrated sulphuric acid is corrosive.

Irritant
– causes reddening
or blistering of skin

Harmful
– damages body
if swallowed,
breathed in or
absorbed through skin

Corrosive
– attacks and destroys
living tissues, including
eyes and skin

The more dilute a solution of acid or alkali is,
the less hazardous it is to use.
However, adding water to concentrated sulphuric acid
is very dangerous. It gives out a lot of energy.
This boils the water, and acid spurts out.

If you spill an acid or alkali in the lab always tell your teacher.
Your teacher will add water and mop up the spill.

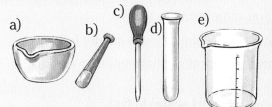

It's a fact!

Drivers who transport acids and alkalis must
carry **Tremcards**. This stands for Transport
Emergency Cards. The cards tell the driver
what to do if there is an emergency.

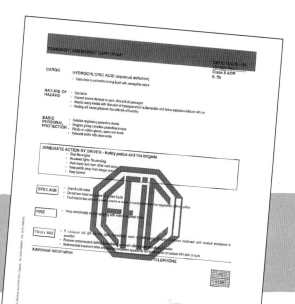

1 Copy the sentences below into your
book filling in the blanks.
Acids are the chemical opposites of . . . .
Indicators are one . . . . in acids and another
. . . . in alkalis.
Litmus is a useful indicator. It turns red in
. . . . and blue in . . . .

2 What do all the alkalis in the picture
at the top of the opposite page have in
common?

3 On the Tremcard for dilute hydrochloric
acid the emergency action for a spillage is:

• Drench with water

• If the substance has entered
a sewer advise police

Why do you think it says this on the
Tremcard?

4 Name these pieces of apparatus.

a) b) c) d) e)

What are a) and b) used for?

5 Write explanations for the following:
a) bottles of hydrochloric acid have
warning labels
b) bottles of lemon juice do not have
warning labels
c) acids are usually kept in glass bottles,
not in metal containers.

6 Think about the practical work you did
in today's lesson. Make a list of things you
did well. Make a list of things you didn't do
well. Write down 2 things you could
improve next time.

Things to do

How strong?

▶ Crack the code to find out what you will be asked to do today! Take:

- The second letter of the word: A rainbow has 7 of these.
- The first letter of the word: The colour of an alkali with litmus.
- The first letter of the word: You wash your hands with this.
- The second letter of the word: An acid you put on pancakes.
- The last letter of the word: It detects acids and alkalis.
- The first letter of the word: An acid served on chips.
- The second letter of the word: The colour of an acid with litmus.

You can use indicators to test for acids and alkalis.

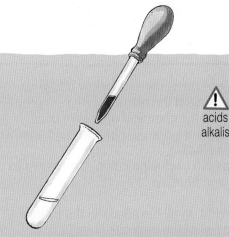

Testing acids and alkalis

Your teacher will give you some solutions and different indicators
to test them with.
Design a table to record colour changes and whether each solution
is acidic or alkaline.
Carry out your tests and fill in your table.

Universal indicator is a mixture of a few indicators. It is very
useful because it tells you how *strong* or *weak* acidic and alkaline
solutions are. You can get universal indicator as a liquid or as paper.

Testing pH

Your teacher will give you some solutions to test.

Put one of the solutions in a test-tube (about a quarter full).

Add a few drops of universal indicator. Shake this tube carefully.
What do you see?

Use the colour chart (called the **pH scale**) to find
the **pH number** of your solution.

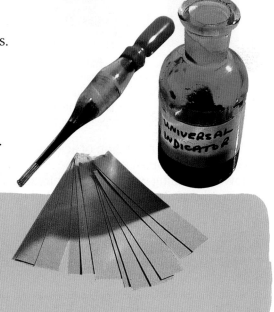

⚠ acids alkalis

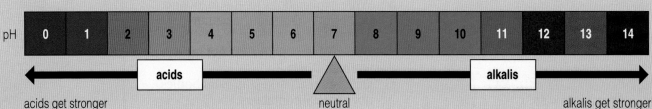

| pH | 0 | 1 | 2 | 3 | 4 | 5 | 6 | 7 | 8 | 9 | 10 | 11 | 12 | 13 | 14 |

◀━━ **acids** ━━━━━━━━△━━━━━━ **alkalis** ━━▶

acids get stronger   neutral   alkalis get stronger

Test the other solutions with universal indicator.

Write down the *colour* and *pH number* each time.
Record whether the solution is an acid or an alkali.

Which is the strongest acid? Which is the strongest alkali?

Substance	Colour	pH	Acid or alkali?

Acid rain

Have you heard about the ***acid rain*** problem? When fuels burn they make gases which move into the air. Some of these gases can form acids – they are acidic. The gases dissolve in water in the clouds. When it rains the acids are brought back to earth. Acid rain can damage buildings and trees. It affects our **environment**.

Trees damaged by acid rain

Stonework damaged by acid rain

Carry out this investigation to see how acid rain affects stonework.

Add a few drops of acid to some crushed limestone.
Write down what you see.

What do you think would happen if you used a weaker acid?
Write down what you expect to see.

Now try it with the weaker acid.

Was your prediction correct?

Do you think acid rain is a strong or weak acid? Why?

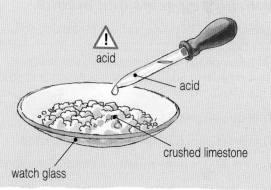

1 Match each of these pH numbers with the correct statement.
pH6   strong acid
pH1   strong alkali
pH14   weak acid
pH8   weak alkali

2 Copy and complete this sentence.
Universal indicator is more useful than litmus because . . . .

3 Answer the following questions about acid rain.
a) Look at the photograph at the top of this page and describe what acid rain does to trees.
b) Write down 3 ways in which humans could make less acid rain
c) Look at your answer to b). Draw a poster to get the message across.

4 Kate says "I think milk gets more acidic if it is left out of the fridge for a long time."
Do you think she is right? Plan an investigation to test Kate's idea.

5 How could you use the crushed limestone and acid test to put 4 acids in order of their strength?

Things to do

A balancing act

Learn about:
● changing the pH of solutions
● making a neutral solution

▶ Look back to the pH chart on page 66. Find the pH number of a solution which is neither acidic nor alkaline.

a What colour is universal indicator in this solution?

Solutions which are neither acids nor alkalis are **neutral**.

You can make neutral solutions by mixing acids and alkalis together. The acid and alkali can balance each other out.

ACID + ALKALI → NEUTRAL SOLUTION

This is called a **neutralisation** reaction.

Neutralising acids and alkalis

Collect 10 cm³ of dilute sodium hydroxide solution (an alkali) in a small beaker.
Add a few drops of universal indicator solution.
Use a pipette to add dilute hydrochloric acid solution to the alkali.

What do you predict will happen?

What will happen if you add too much acid?

How could you neutralise the solution if you do add too much acid?

Try the experiment and describe what you find out.

▶ Copy the diagrams below into your book. The 3 labels are missing.
Choose the correct labels from the list to complete your diagrams.

- water
- acid
- acid and indicator
- alkali
- neutral solution and indicator
- indicator
- neutral solution
- alkali and indicator

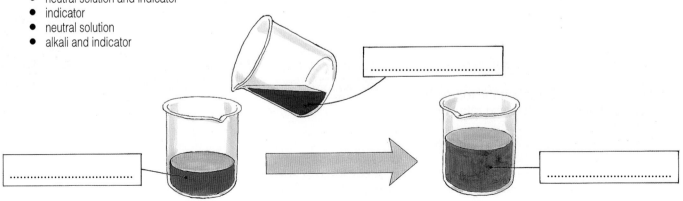

pH sensors

So far we have measured pH using universal indicator.

A more accurate way of measuring the pH of a solution is to use a pH sensor and data-logging equipment.

You can see how the pH changes when we add an acid to an alkali in the next experiment.

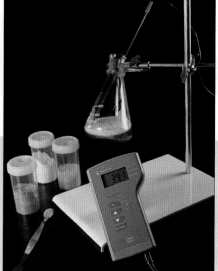

A pH sensor

Monitoring pH changes

Look at the experiment below:

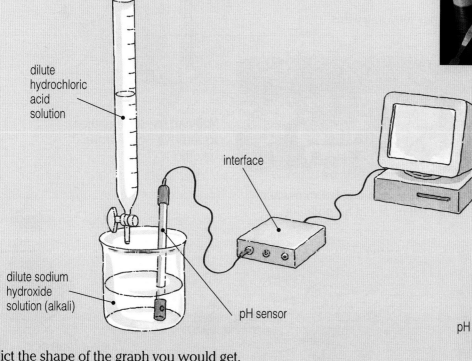

dilute hydrochloric acid solution

interface

dilute sodium hydroxide solution (alkali)

pH sensor

Predict the shape of the graph you would get.
Watch the experiment.
How do you know when 'the point of neutralisation' has been reached?

pH

volume of acid added

Things to do

1 Copy and complete:
A substance with a . . . . number of 4 is an . . . . If a weak . . . . is added to it, the solution can become neutral with a pH number of . . . .
We call this a . . . . reaction.
We can monitor pH changes using a pH . . . .

2 In the last few lessons you have been using different indicators – litmus, universal indicator, and some you made yourself from petals, berries or vegetables.
Why is universal indicator the best one to use when neutralising acids or alkalis?

3 Look at the graph below:

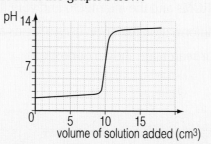

a) Was the solution you started with an acid or an alkali? How can you tell?
b) Was the solution added an acid or alkali?
c) How much solution was needed to get a neutral solution?

Using acids and alkalis

Learn about:
- using acids and alkalis
- neutralisations

pH all around you

▶ In your group discuss the following pictures.

- Decide whether you all agree with the statements.
- Choose one statement to test. What would you do?
- If there is time, your teacher may let you try this.

You can use lemon juice to remove 'scale' from a kettle.

If we measure the pH of rainwater, it can tell us about air pollution.

All shampoos are pH balanced.

Acid drop sweets are not really acids.

acid

Vinegar is an acid. It should carry a hazard warning.

Researching acids and alkalis

Find out more about the uses of acids and alkalis.
You can use books, videos, ROMs and the internet to find your information.

Present your findings as an information folder on uses of acids and alkalis.

Some key words to start your search are shown opposite.

digestion

skin creams

shampoos

acidic soil

preserving food

insect bites and stings

soaps

It's a fact!

The bacteria in your mouth can change sugary food into acid. If the acid stays in your mouth for a long time, it attacks your teeth. This causes tooth decay. Toothpastes often contain weak alkali to neutralise acid in the mouth.

Neutralising your stomach!

Did you know that there is acid in your stomach?

Have you ever had a stomach ache? Sometimes this can be caused by your stomach making too much acid.

Indigestion tablets or stomach powders can be used to 'settle' your stomach.

Do you think these tablets and powders are acids, alkalis or neutral? Why?

▶ Have you seen any advertisements about curing indigestion? Write down the names of some cures.

SCI-CO HEALTHCARE

Your health is our care

MEMO TO: *Analysts*   FROM: *Chris Williams*

The company wishes to test three stomach powders, A, B and C, to see how well they neutralise stomach acid.

Please carry out some tests to tell me how much of each powder you need to neutralise the stomach acid. Make sure you do fair tests. Be as accurate as possible.

Our first tests show that one powder will not work at all. Please check this. I'd like a report on:

(a) how you carried out the tests - including all measurements you made

(b) your results

(c) which powder is best at neutralising stomach acid.

This is urgent! Thanks.

Things to do

1 This question is about some uses of acids and alkalis.
a) Which acid is used to preserve pickled onions?
b) How would you soothe the pain from an alkaline wasp sting?
c) How do farmers neutralise soil that is acidic?
d) A shampoo has a pH of 5.6 – is it acidic or alkaline?

2 Acid can cause tooth decay! Design and make a leaflet to tell young children about the need to brush teeth regularly.

3 Find out about some medicines used to treat stomach acid and indigestion.
a) Make a list of their ingredients.
b) Are there any chemicals in common? If so, give their names.
c) List the medicines by name in a table.

Tablet	Powder	Liquid

d) Medicines can be sold as tablets, powder or liquid. Write down an advantage of each of these.
e) What other things would you consider before choosing a medicine to cure indigestion?

Questions

1 Design and make a poster to explain the word *acid*.
Use key words and clear drawings.

2 Indicators can be made by crushing some plants and vegetables with a liquid. You can use propanone or methylated spirit to make an indicator with red cabbage.
Jill says that propanone is better at removing the colour.
Plan an investigation to see if she is right.

Red cabbages make good indicators

3 Write a report on the different uses of acids in the home.

4 Make a list of all the chemical indicators you have used in this topic.
Which indicator was the most useful? Why?

5 Read the letter to a newspaper shown here. Write a reply to Mr. Clark. Say whether you agree or disagree with his ideas.

> I'm fed up with all these chemical tankers on our roads. Many of them carry dangerous things such as acids. Any spills from the tankers could kill people. I think tankers should only be allowed to use the roads between 11 pm and 6 am. Then there are fewer cars around. I want the government to make this law. Will others support me?
> **Mr. C. Clark**

6 A local farmer wants to neutralise his acidic soil. He cannot decide whether to use CALCOLIME or SUPERCAL for this.
a) Plan an investigation to find out which is better at neutralising the soil.
b) What other factors should the farmer consider before choosing which to use?

7 If you leave a half-eaten apple in the air it goes brown.
Keeping pieces of apple in a solution of lemon juice slows down the rate of browning.
Do you think this could be something to do with the pH of the solution?
Make a prediction.
Plan an investigation to test your prediction.

8 Acids and alkalis can be dangerous substances.
You must be careful when you use them.
Design a warning poster for your laboratory.

Chemical reactions

Everything around us is made of materials. Some are found naturally. Some need to be made from raw materials.

The 'made materials' will come from chemical reactions.

What would your life be like without …
glass, plastic, metals … ?

In this unit:

New materials

Some materials are **natural**. Others are **made**.

The wool from a sheep is a **natural** material.
Why is it useful?

The wood from a tree is a **natural** material.
Why is it useful?

Sometimes scientists need to *make* the useful materials.
The material made is **synthetic**.

Glass is a **synthetic** material.
It can be made from sand, limestone and sodium carbonate.
It is made in a **chemical reaction**.

A **property** of glass is that it is transparent.
This means it is useful for making windows.

(Remember that a **property** must describe *any* piece
of the material.)

Just the job!

Some of the clothes you wear are made
from natural materials. Examples are
cotton, wool and silk.
Other clothes are made from **synthetic**
(made) materials. Examples are polyester
and acrylic.
You may have some clothes made of a
mixture of materials. An example is polyester
and cotton.

Different materials have different properties.
Look at the pictures here. For each one, say
which properties the material used for the
clothing should have.

Example:
Ideally T-shirts should be made of material
which is light and lets body heat out.

Making new substances always involves a **chemical reaction**.
How do we know when a reaction has taken place?

Recognising reactions

Try out the following reactions:

⚠ eye protection

- lemon juice and bicarbonate of soda (in a beaker).

- baking powder and water (in a beaker).

- plaster of Paris and water (in a yoghurt pot, using an ice-lolly stick to stir the mixture).

Record any observations and look for signs of chemical reactions.
Are new substances formed? How do you know? Are there changes in temperature?

Reacting metals with acids

Try out the reaction shown.
Test the gas collected with a lighted splint.

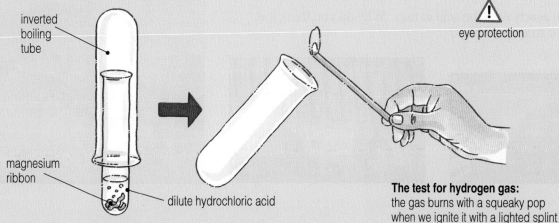

inverted boiling tube

⚠ eye protection

magnesium ribbon

dilute hydrochloric acid

The test for hydrogen gas:
the gas burns with a squeaky pop
when we ignite it with a lighted splint

What are the signs that the magnesium and acid react together?

Try out a range of other metals with different acids.
Design a table to record your results.
Look for any patterns.

What gas is given off when a metal reacts with an acid?
Do all metals react with acids?

Things to do

1 What are the signs of a chemical reaction?
Make a list of things you might notice.

2 Use books or ROMs to find out some properties of hydrogen gas.

3 Copy the table into your book. Write down 3 materials in each column.

Natural	Synthetic (made)

4 Do a survey of your clothes at home.
- Look at the label to see what your clothes are made of.
- What does the material feel like? (soft, rough, smooth, etc.)
- Are there any special care instructions, e.g. for washing or drying?
Record your findings in a table.
From your list say:
a) which material can be washed at the highest temperature?
b) which material feels the roughest?

A race against time!

Learn about:
- testing for carbon dioxide
- patterns and generalisations

▶ Look at these photographs. They show a gargoyle at Lincoln Cathedral. They were taken 100 years apart.

a Which photo was taken most recently?

b What has caused the gargoyle to change over the years?

Lots of buildings are made of limestone.
Limestone contains a substance called *calcium carbonate*.
It reacts with acid to make carbon dioxide.

c Limestone reacts with the acid in rain. Why do you think it is still used to make buildings?

Calcium carbonate plus acid

You can test the gas given off when calcium carbonate reacts with acid.

We use lime water to test for carbon dioxide gas.

Carbon dioxide turns lime water milky/cloudy.

Try the experiment below:

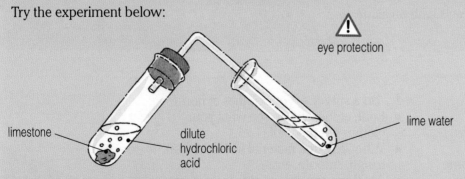

⚠ eye protection

limestone

dilute hydrochloric acid

lime water

How do you know that a chemical reaction is taking place?

Now try out some other carbonates and different acids.
Record your results in a table.

What pattern can you see? Do all carbonates react with acids?
Is carbon dioxide always given off?

Watching an acid attack!

Your teacher will show you limestone and acid reacting in the apparatus opposite.

But before the experiment starts, make a prediction.
Do you think the mass of the flask and its contents will change during the reaction?
Will the mass . . . stay the same?
          . . . go up?
          . . . go down?
Predict what you think will happen. Why?

We can use an electronic balance to measure mass.
The electronic balance can be linked to a computer.
The computer will record the mass.

On paper sketch the shape of the graph you expect to see.
(Do not mark this book.)

Your teacher will now add the limestone to the acid.

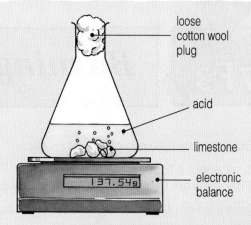

loose
cotton wool
plug

acid

limestone

electronic
balance

137.54g

mass
in
grams

time in seconds

d   What happens to the mass of the flask and its contents?

e   Why do you think this happens?

f   Is this a fast or slow reaction?

g   Why do you think the reaction at Lincoln Cathedral is slower?

h   Why do we use a loose cotton wool plug in the experiment?

---

1   Jan wants to make and collect a sample of carbon dioxide gas.
a) Draw a labelled diagram of the apparatus she could use.
b) Why can you collect carbon dioxide **over water**?
What does this tell you about the gas?
c) How could Jan test the gas to show it is carbon dioxide gas?
Draw a diagram of the apparatus.
Describe what she would see.

2   Carbon dioxide is the 'fizz' in fizzy drinks.

Find out 2 other uses of carbon dioxide.

3   When magnesium ribbon reacts with an acid, it makes hydrogen gas. Ben measured the volume of gas given off every minute.

Time (minutes)	Volume (cm³)
0	0
1	20
2	35
3	45
4	50
5	52
6	52
7	52
8	52

a) Draw a graph of these results.

volume

time

b) After how many minutes had the reaction finished?
c) What volume of hydrogen had been collected at the end of the reaction?
d) When was the reaction fastest . . . near the start or near the end?

Things to do

Burning

Learn about:
- the process of burning
- the formation of oxides
- word equations

Burning is an example of a chemical reaction.

▶ Think about a burning piece of paper.
What signs are there that a reaction is taking place?

▶ Make a list of other burning reactions you have seen.

Burning is a chemical reaction

Investigating burning

Set up the experiment below:

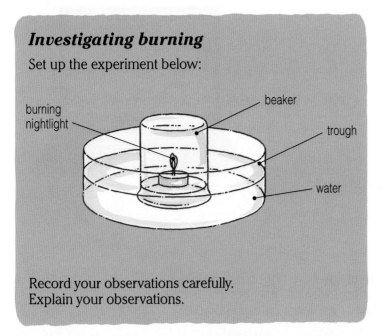

Record your observations carefully.
Explain your observations.

Have you ever burnt the toast?

For materials to burn we need **oxygen** gas.
The air contains about 21% oxygen.

▶ What do you think will happen if we burn things in *pure* oxygen?

How should you deal with a chip pan fire?

Burning in oxygen

Watch your teacher burn some substances in oxygen gas.
Record your observations in a table.
Make a list of the safety precautions taken.

The new substances made are called **oxides**.

We can show what happens in a reaction in a **word equation**.
For example:

magnesium + oxygen ⟶ magnesium oxide
reactants ⟶ **product**

A word equation shows the substances we start with (reactants)
and the new substances formed (products).

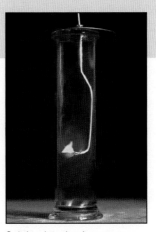

Sulphur burning in oxygen

Burning candles . . . what do you think?

A candle is made of wax. It contains **carbon** and **hydrogen**.

⚠️ eye protection

1. Predict what will happen when a beaker is put over a burning candle in a sand tray.
   What do you expect to see?

   Now try the experiment. Were you right?

2. A more difficult prediction . . .
   Predict what will happen when a beaker is put over candles of three different heights.
   Which candle do you think will go out first?
   Explain your ideas.

   Now try the experiment. Were you right?
   Try to explain what happened.

candle wax + oxygen ———→ carbon dioxide + water + energy

This reaction is an example of an **oxidation**.
A substance has **gained** oxygen.

3. Plan an investigation to find out how the volume of air in a beaker affects the time a candle burns.

   Predict what you expect will happen.

   How will you measure the volume of air in a beaker?

   How will you make your timings reliable?

   How will you record your results?

   What type of graph will you use to show any pattern?

   Let your teacher check your plan before you start your tests.

   Evaluate your investigation.

---

1 Explain these words:
a) reactant   c) word equation
b) product   d) oxide

2 a) How much gas will be left if a substance burns in 200 cm³ of air (assume that all the oxygen is used up and air contains about 21% oxygen)?
b) Which gas makes up most of the air?

3 Fill in the gaps in these word equations:
a) copper + ... ——→ copper oxide
b) .... + oxygen ——→ sodium oxide
c) .... + ... ——→ carbon dioxide
d) iron + oxygen ——→ ....
e) sulphur + ... ——→ .... dioxide
f) hydrogen + ... ——→ water
g) What is the chemical name for water?

Things to do

Learn about:
- fuels releasing energy
- products of combustion

Have you ever seen this symbol?
This is called the **fire triangle**.

a Why are the words HEAT, OXYGEN and FUEL written on the fire triangle?

b Use the fire triangle to explain what you must do to stop a fire.

A fuel is a substance which burns in oxygen to give us energy.
New substances are made as the fuel burns.

▶ Make a list of all the fuels you can think of.
Choose 3 which you think are the most important. Explain why.

Burning is a **chemical reaction**. The reaction is between the fuel and the oxygen gas in the air.
This chemical change is also called **combustion**.
When the fuel burns it makes **oxides**.

fuel + oxygen ⟶ oxides + energy

This is an **exothermic** reaction.
This means heat (energy) is given out.

A Bunsen burner uses natural gas

Burning a fuel

Bread is an example of a fuel. It is fuel for your body.
Usually you don't want to burn the toast. But in the next experiment you will do just that!

Hold the bread in tongs over a heat-resistant mat.
Observe the bread very carefully.
Heat the bread until it no longer burns.
Write down everything you see.

⚠ eye protection

What happens to the bread during burning?

In your group, discuss your ideas about burning.

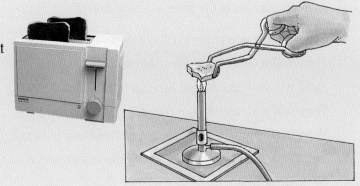

 Bread is like most fuels. It contains hydrogen and carbon. That must mean it makes oxides of carbon and hydrogen when it burns.  Where do the oxides go?

c When carbon reacts with oxygen it makes . . . .

d When hydrogen reacts with oxygen it makes . . . . This is usually called . . . .

e Where *do* the substances made in **c** and **d** go?

Testing the products of combustion

Before we can test the gases given off when we burn a fuel, we need to know the test for water:

water turns white anhydrous copper sulphate blue.

Bunsen burners usually use natural gas as a fuel.

Natural gas is made up mainly of methane gas. Like other fossil fuels, natural gas contains lots of carbon and hydrogen.

Watch as your teacher carries out the experiment below.

How do you test for carbon dioxide and water?

How do we know we are making these substances?

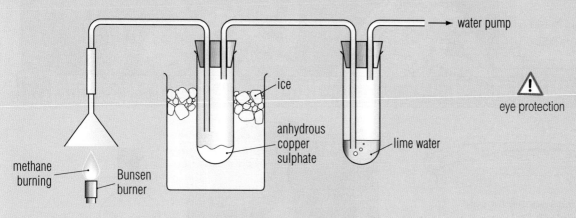

What do you observe?
Explain your observations.

When we burn the fuel, methane, we get:

methane + oxygen ⟶ carbon dioxide + water

This is the word equation for the combustion of methane.

---

1 Write 2 or 3 lines about each of the following words to explain what it means.
a) fuel   c) combustion
b) fire triangle   d) methane

2 You need to take great care when using fuels. Make a leaflet for the fire brigade to warn people of the dangers.

3 Ethanol is a substance which is made from carbon, hydrogen and oxygen. Copy and complete the word equation to show what you think happens when it burns.

ethanol + ... ⟶ .... + water

4 Collect some newspaper cuttings about fires. For each fire try to find out:
a) How the fire started.
b) Whether the fire could have been prevented.
c) How the fire was put out.
Record all the information in a table.

5 Fuels can be solids, liquids or gases. Give one example of each type.
What are the advantages of
a) a **solid** fuel?
b) a **liquid** fuel?
c) a **gaseous** fuel?

Things to do

A burning tale

500 B.C.

The Greeks thought that the universe was made from 4 things: fire, water, air and earth.
They believed **everything** was made of these substances.

So what happens when something burns?

The fire is released.

The water and air escape

The earth or ashes are left behind.

EARTH
AIR · FIRE
WATER

For over 2000 years people thought these were good ideas.
Then in the 1600s some scientists began to think about it again.
They thought that burning depended on the air.
But they believed the air was one single substance.

Robert Boyle heated some tin in a sealed flask. When the seal was broken, the tin weighed more than before heating.
Boyle thought the particles of fire had lodged between the particles of tin.

Georg Stahl (1660–1734) was a German scientist. He developed another idea. It was called the phlogiston theory (from the Greek phlox = flame).

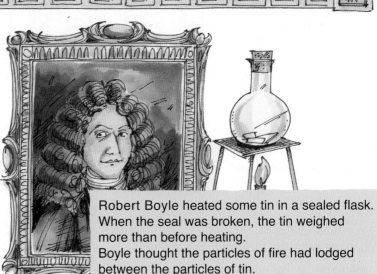

But this burnt charcoal has only left a little ash.

That's because it contains so much PHLOGISTON!

Every substance that burns has 2 parts — ash and PHLOGISTON.

When something burns the PHLOGISTON escapes. The ash is left behind.

In the early 1700s, the phlogiston theory was thought to be a great idea. But it didn't explain everything. Many materials like Boyle's tin, **gained** weight after heating. They should have been **losing** phlogiston. The theory must be wrong.

Antoine Lavoisier was a French scientist. He worked with his wife. Together they worked on the problem of burning. They knew the phlogiston theory wasn't quite right.

Something is wrong here!

Lavoisier heated sulphur. He found that the sulphur gained weight when it burnt. He thought the air was combining with the sulphur. But it needed a visit from **Joseph Priestley** in 1774 to help Lavoisier to understand.

This is the piece of apparatus Lavoisier used for his early burning experiments. How do you think it works?

Joseph Priestley worked in England. He heated mercury in air. He made a red substance. When he heated the red substance he got a new gas.

Priestley went to France to tell Lavoisier about the gas. Lavoisier repeated and improved Priestley's experiments. He soon understood the results. Air must be more than one gas. One gas is needed for burning. This is oxygen.

This gas lets things burn very brightly in it.

When a substance burns it combines with oxygen in the air.

MERCU

Things to do

1 Read about Robert Boyle's experiment.
a) Suppose Boyle had reweighed his heated flask **before** breaking the seal. What do you think he would have found?
b) Why did the flask weigh more **after** the seal was broken?

2 Supporters of the phlogiston theory argued strongly with those who disagreed. Write a cartoon strip to show an argument between 2 scientists in the 1700s. One scientist believes the phlogiston theory, the other does not.

3 Lavoisier was working during the French Revolution. Find out what life was like in France at this time. What problems would scientists have had?

4 Lavoisier was sentenced to death after the French Revolution. He had become a hated tax collector for the government. Revolutionaries wanted him dead. The judge said "The Republic has no need of men of science." Do you think your country has "no need of scientists?" Explain your views.

5 Lavoisier found that only some of the air was used up when mercury was heated in air.
a) Design some apparatus which he could have used to show this.
b) What percentage of the air is oxygen?
c) Oxygen is a very useful gas. How is pure oxygen separated from the air?

Questions

1 Zinc reacts with dilute sulphuric acid.
  a) How can you see that a chemical reaction takes place?
  b) Name the reactants.
  c) One product formed in the reaction is called zinc sulphate. Name the other product.
  d) How would you test for this other product named in part c)?
  e) Write a word equation to show the reaction between zinc and sulphuric acid.
  f) Name one metal that will **not** react with dilute sulphuric acid.

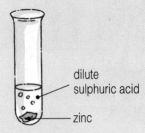

dilute sulphuric acid

zinc

2 Jason thinks that the gas given off when you add water to baking powder is carbon dioxide.
  a) Draw the apparatus Jason could use to test for carbon dioxide.
  b) Write down the result of the test.

3 a) Which are the two main gases in the air?
  b) Design an experiment to find out how much oxygen is in the air. (The diagram opposite might give you a clue about one possible way.)

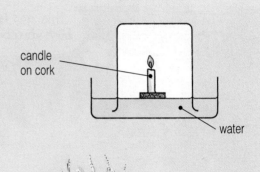

candle on cork

water

4

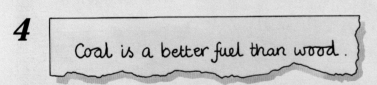

Coal is a better fuel than wood.

  a) Do you think this statement is correct?
  b) What makes a good fuel?
    What tests could you do to see which fuel is better?
  c) How can you test if carbon dioxide and water are formed when wood burns?

5 The UK chemical industry is the 5th largest in the world. It makes many different products.
Draw a bar-chart or a pie-chart of these data:

Products made	Percentage of the industry (%)
Fertilisers	8
Organic materials	12
Inorganic materials	7
Soaps and toiletries	9
Pharmaceuticals	24
Plastics and rubbers	5
Paints and varnishes	8
Dyes and pigments	4
Specialised chemical products	23

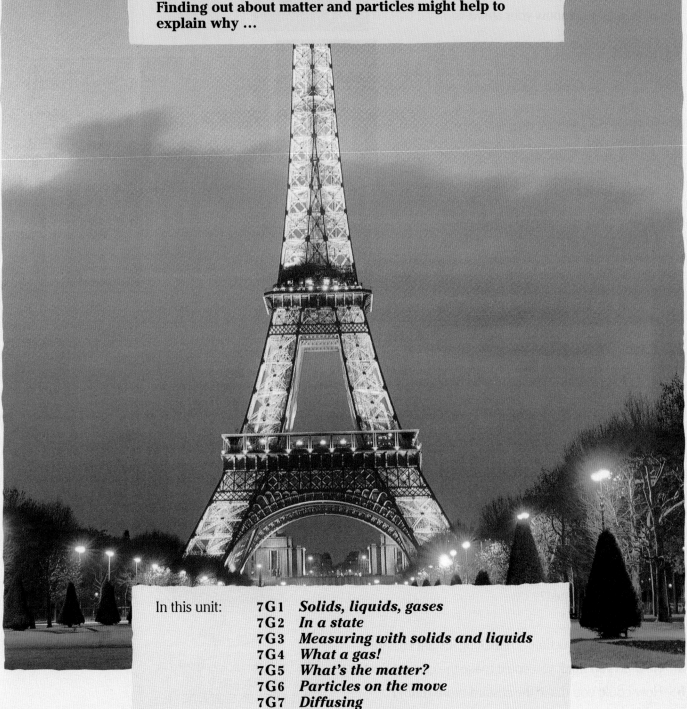

The Eiffel Tower in Paris is about 300 metres high.
But did you know its height can change?
In summer it is taller than in winter.
The difference can be 10 cm.
Finding out about matter and particles might help to explain why …

In this unit:

Solids, liquids, gases

▶ Look at these photographs of substances you might find at home.

Which are solids? Which are liquids? Which are gases?

Make a table to show your answers.

You might be able to tell easily which things are solids, which are liquids and which are gases. It can be hard to explain **how** you can tell!

▶ Observe the samples your teacher will give you.
In your group write down some differences between the way solids, liquids and gases behave.

Make a table to show your answers. These are the **properties** of solids, liquids and gases.

Some substances are difficult to classify.

Think about custard!

You can have liquid custard.
It's easy to pour.
It can be stirred.
It takes the shape of its container.

When custard sets it behaves like a solid.
It cannot be poured.
It cannot be stirred.
It has its own shape.

Is custard solid or liquid?

▶ Look at the instructions for making instant custard:

a How do you think you could make the custard thicker?

b How could you make the custard more runny?

c How could you make sure the custard is smooth?

Empty one sachet into a measuring jug.
Add BOILING WATER to $\frac{3}{4}$ pint (425 ml) mark.

Looking at solids, liquids and gases

Squashing

* Put the top tightly on a plastic bottle filled with air.
  Squeeze the bottle with your hands.
  Can you squash the bottle inwards?

* Now fill the plastic bottle with water.
  Put the top on tightly again.
  Try to squeeze the bottle.

* Take a piece of rock. Squeeze it with your hands.

d What do you notice? Try to explain your results.

e What do they tell you about solids, liquids and gases?

Watching

* Drop a crystal in a beaker of **cold** water.
  Drop another crystal in a beaker of **hot** water.
  Leave them for a while. Watch.

f What do you notice? Try to explain your results.

g What do they tell you about solids and liquids?

Smelling

* Take the top off the bottle your teacher will give you.
  Hold it 10 cm away from you.

h What do you notice? Try to explain your results.

i What do they tell you about gases?

* Discuss your explanations with another group.

j Did other people have different ideas to you?
In what ways have you changed your ideas, if at all?

▶ Look at your table about how solids, liquids and gases behave.
Can you add some more ideas to the table now?
Try making a key you could use to decide if a material is a solid,
a liquid or a gas.

---

1 Fill in the blanks with either 'liquids' or 'solids'.

.... are runny.
.... are hard.
.... can be poured.
.... take the shape of the container.
.... cannot be stirred.
.... have a fixed shape.
.... and .... cannot be easily squashed.

2 Some substances are difficult to classify as liquids or solids. Custard is one example. Write down 3 other examples.

3 Write a paragraph about liquids. Include the following words:

wet	pour	thick	thin	drip
	flow	container	freeze	

4 Write a paragraph about gases. Include the following words:

squash	air	smell	light
	fizzy	balloon	

Things to do

In a state

You can describe substances as **solids**, **liquids** and **gases**.
These are the 3 **states of matter**.

Particles

You have already seen that solids, liquids and gases behave in different ways.

We can explain the differences using a theory.
Scientists believe that everything is made of tiny **particles**.

In solids, liquids and gases the particles are arranged in different ways.

The 3 drawings opposite represent the 3 ways:

Which is
. . .the solid?
. . .the liquid?
. . .the gas?

▶ In your group discuss which drawing represents:
- a solid
- a liquid
- a gas.

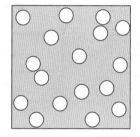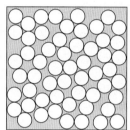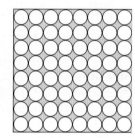

Your table of solid, liquid and gas properties should help you to decide.

Check your ideas with those of another group.

▶ Copy the particle arrangements shown above.
Label each one as either solid, liquid or gas.

Do you think particles move   … in solids?
  … in liquids?
  … in gases?

Give reasons for your ideas.
Does everyone agree?

Warming a solid

What happens to the length of a wire when it is heated?

Predict what will happen in the experiment shown opposite.

Now try it out.

⚠ Care – hot wires can burn.

Warm the wire with a Bunsen burner.

What happens to the length of the wire?

Use the idea of **particles** to explain what you see.

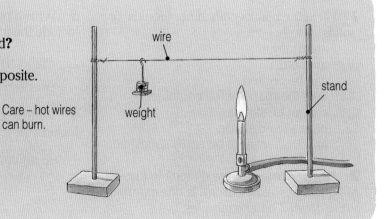

Warming a liquid

Fill a test-tube with water.
Put a rubber stopper and glass tube in it, as shown in the diagram opposite.
Mark the water level above the stopper.

Predict what will happen when the tube is put in a beaker of hot water.

Now try it out.

What happens to the volume of a liquid when it is warmed?

What happens when the liquid is cooled again?

Use the idea of **particles** to explain what you see.

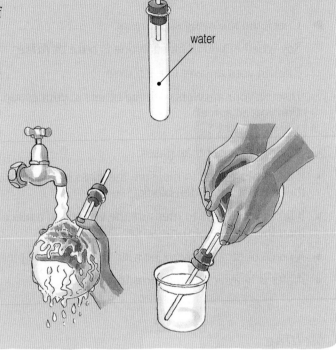

water

Warming a gas

Predict what you think will happen in this experiment.

Take a flask fitted with a stopper and a glass tube.
Run cold water on to the outside for 3 minutes.
Put the glass tube into a beaker of water.
Warm the outside of the flask with your hands.

Now try the experiment.

Use the idea of **particles** to explain what you see.

When things get bigger, we say they **expand**.
When things get smaller, we say they **contract**.

Gases, liquids and solids *expand* when heated.

a Which expands most, a gas, a liquid or a solid?

> **Remember!**
> The particles themselves **do not** expand or contract as the temperature changes.

Things to do

1 Copy and complete using some of the words in the box:

melting	lumps	large	small
solids	gases	liquids	particles
same	contract	hot	expand

a) The three states of matter are . . . . , ... and . . . .
b) . . . . and . . . . are harder to compress (squeeze together) than . . . .
c) Everything is made of . . . .
d) The particles are very . . . .
e) Oven shelves fit more tightly in . . . . ovens.
f) Gases, liquids and solids . . . . when warmed.

2 Which of the following is the best substance to use to fill bicycle tyres? Why?

water	compressed air	wood

3 The label on a lemonade bottle shows the contents:

> water, citric acid, flavourings, carbon dioxide, artificial sweetener

a) Name one substance in the list that is:
   i) a liquid   ii) a gas.
b) There is normally a lot of sugar in fizzy drinks. Which substance in the list replaces sugar?
c) Why do you think that sugar is not used here?
d) Is sugar a solid, liquid or gas?

Measuring with solids and liquids

Learn about:
- changes of state
- applying particle theory to explain observations

▶ Check the following statements.

Say whether you think each one is *true* or *false*.

Explain your answer in each case.

Discuss your answers with the others in your group. Can you all agree?

- Solids are denser than gases.
- It takes more time to measure the mass of shampoo than the mass of a wooden block.
- It takes more time to measure the volume of a piece of rock than the volume of some water.
- A piece of rock is always heavier than a piece of plastic.
- Water is heavier when it turns to solid ice.

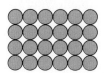
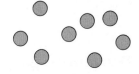

Are solids denser than gases?

Melting

If you heat a solid, you can turn it into a liquid. We say that the solid **melts**.

▶ Make a list of 6 things you have seen melt, e.g. butter, …

The temperature when a solid melts (turns to liquid) is called the **melting point**.

This is the same temperature as when the liquid freezes (turns to solid).

This temperature is also called the **freezing point**.

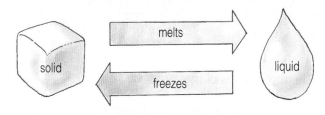

solid — melts → liquid
liquid — freezes → solid

▶ Look at the melting point values in the table.

a Which substance has the lowest melting point?

b Which substance has the highest melting point?

c In cold weather, which freezes first, water or alcohol?

d Room temperature is about 25 °C. Which of these substances may be liquids at this temperature? Why can't you be sure?

e On being heated from room temperature, which melts first, aluminium or copper?

f What happens if you keep heating a liquid?

g What happens to the particles when a solid melts?

Substance	Melting point in °C
aluminium	660
ice	0
alcohol	−117
iron	1535
copper	1083
mercury	−39
polythene	110

Why do we put salt on roads in winter?

To answer this question you could use some temperature sensors.

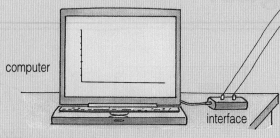

computer

interface

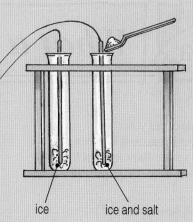

ice   ice and salt

- Place the sensors on the desk carefully.
- Get 2 boiling tubes. Put 10 g of crushed ice into each.
- Add 0.2 g of salt to one tube and stir to mix the ice and salt completely.
- Quickly put one temperature sensor in each tube.
  Make sure it is in the centre of the crushed ice. Wait 1 minute.
- Record the temperature of the ice for 20 minutes.
- Watch the ice carefully.
  Record any changes in its appearance over the 20 minutes.

Draw or print out the graph to show how the temperature changes.
Mark on your graph the point at which the ice melted.

h At the start, what was the ***state*** of the ice?

i What happened to the solid ice after a while?

j Are the graphs for 'ice on its own' and 'ice and salt' different in any way?

k Describe the shape of the graphs. Which part of the graphs is surprising?

l What effect does salt have on ice?

m Why is salt put on roads in winter?

---

1 Copy and complete each of these statements using one of the words in brackets at the end.
a) Solids are . . . . dense than gases.
   (less/more)
b) The . . . . when a solid melts is called the melting point. (temperature/time)
c) The . . . . of a liquid is measured in cm³.
   (mass/volume)
d) When a solid melts it forms . . . .
   (ice/liquid)
e) When a liquid freezes it turns to
   . . . . (solid/gas)

2 Cooking oil and alcohol expand when they are heated.
Design an investigation to see which liquid expands more.

3 Explain how you can measure the density of a piece of rock.

$$\left(\text{density} = \frac{\text{mass}}{\text{volume}}\right)$$

Use diagrams to help you explain.

4 Explain why ***liquids*** are used in thermometers.

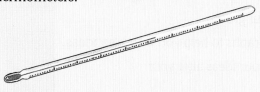

5 Use the information in the melting point table on page 90 to draw a bar-chart.
Organize the substances in melting point order for your bar-chart.

Things to do

What a gas!

Gases are all around you.
The air you are breathing is a gas.
Gases fill any space they are put into.
Gases are made when liquids boil.

$$\text{LIQUID} \xrightarrow[\text{condenses}]{\text{boils}} \text{GAS}$$

The temperature when a liquid boils is called the **boiling point**.

▶ Some gases are listed in the box opposite.
What do you know about them?
Make a patterned note to show your ideas.
You could start like this:

Gases
hydrogen
oxygen
air
nitrogen
carbon dioxide
chlorine
helium
neon
ozone
carbon monoxide
argon

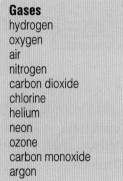

Use books and ROMs to find extra information.

Air is about $\frac{4}{5}$th nitrogen and $\frac{1}{5}$th oxygen. There are also small amounts of other gases such as carbon dioxide and argon.

Gases are much lighter than solids and liquids.
Different gases have different masses.
Nitrogen is slightly lighter than oxygen. Hydrogen is a very light gas.
Carbon dioxide is a heavy gas.

Where is the air?

▶ You cannot see the gases in the air.
How do you know the air is all around you?

Discuss this in your group.

Use these photographs to help you with your ideas.

Did you change your ideas after your discussions?

Where is the air?

Making oxygen

The most important gas in the air is **oxygen**.
We need it to breathe. It keeps us alive.

In this experiment you can make some oxygen gas.
You can also test to prove it is there!

Your teacher will show you how to
'collect a gas over water'.

- Put 2 spatula measures of the black
  powder into a conical flask.

- Fit a stopper, a thistle funnel and a
  delivery tube into the flask, as shown in
  the diagram.

- Fill some test-tubes with water.
  You will use these to collect the oxygen.

- Set up your apparatus to collect the gas.

- Pour hydrogen peroxide down the thistle
  funnel.
  ***Do not collect the first few bubbles
  of gas. Why not?***

- Collect 2 or 3 tubes of oxygen gas.
  Put a stopper in each tube.
  Put the tubes in a test-tube rack.

- Light a spill.
  Blow it out so that the tip is glowing.

- Put the glowing spill inside the tube.
  What do you see?

- Draw a picture to show how the particles
  are arranged in the oxygen.

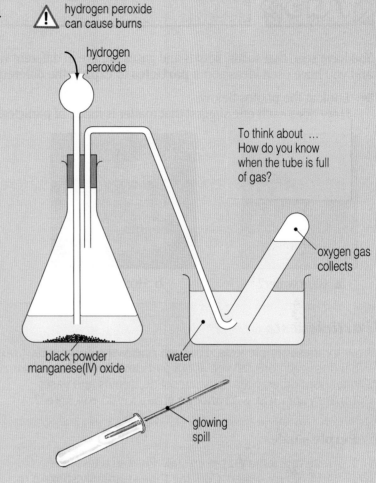

hydrogen peroxide
can cause burns

hydrogen
peroxide

To think about …
How do you know
when the tube is full
of gas?

oxygen gas
collects

black powder
manganese(IV) oxide

water

glowing
spill

---

1 Copy and complete:
a) The air is made up of 2 main gases
   called . . . . and . . . .
b) . . . . is the gas we use to breathe.
c) We breathe out a gas called . . . . dioxide.
d) Hydrogen is a very . . . . gas.
e) We cannot describe the shape of a gas
   because . . . .

2 Laura has drunk all the lemonade in her
bottle. She says the bottle is empty.
Is she right?

3 Which is heavier?

air   oxygen

Explain your idea.

4 Jill has 3 balloons which are filled with
different gases.
Which balloon holds:
a) air?
b) helium?
c) carbon dioxide?

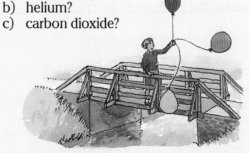

5 Draw a pie-chart to show the
composition of the air.
Label the sections 'oxygen', 'nitrogen' and
'other gases'.

Things to do

What's the matter?

Learn about:
● applying particle theory to explain results

You have seen that solids, liquids and gases behave in different ways and you have used ideas about **particles** to explain the differences.

▶ Look at the photos below.
How does each one suggest that matter is made of particles?

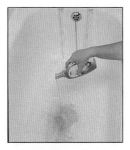

a Blue water? **b** Hot curry? **c** Sweet mug? **d** Lovely smell?

Particle tests

Now try these simple tests. For each one, write down what you notice.
What does each one tell you about particles? Write down your ideas.
Think about differences between solids, liquids and gases.
Compare your ideas with another group's – do you agree?

Purple shades

1. Take one large purple crystal. Put it in a test-tube.
   Add 10 cm³ water. Cork the tube. Carefully shake it to dissolve the crystal.

2. Take 1 cm³ of this solution in another test-tube.
   Add 9 cm³ water. Cork the tube. Carefully shake it.

3. Repeat step 2 again and again. Do this until you can't see the pink colour any more.

⚠ crystal harmful if swallowed

How many times did you repeat step 2?
What does this tell you about the particles in the crystal?

Lost in spaces?

Measure 25 cm³ sand in a measuring cylinder.
Measure 25 cm³ dried peas in another cylinder.
Predict the total volume when the 2 solids are added together and mixed.

Now mix the 2 solids. Shake the substances well.
Let the mixture settle.
What is the ***total*** volume?

Warm air

Watch your teacher gently warm a tube of air?
What do you see?

As soon as heating stops, the delivery tube must be
lifted out of the water? Why?

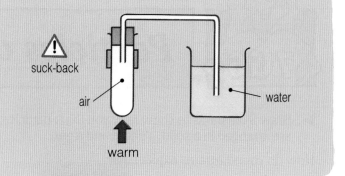

'Dry ice'

Have you seen 'dry ice' being used at pop concerts?
'Dry ice' is solid carbon dioxide.
The solid turns easily to gas. It is stored in pressurised containers.

A **small** volume of solid gives a **large** volume of gas.
e　What does this tell you about particles in solids and gases?

Rising balloons

A balloon rises if it is less dense than the air around it.

f　How does the air in a hot-air balloon become less dense than
the air outside?
Try to explain your idea by drawing particles.

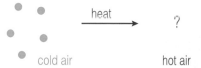

1　Copy and complete.
Choose the correct word from the 2 in
brackets.
a)　All matter is made of . . . .
(particles/solids)
b)　The particles are very . . . . (small/large)
c)　In a gas, the particles are . . . . (more/less)
spread out than in a liquid.

2　Soluble aspirin tablets are used to treat
headaches.

What happens to the particles in the tablet
when it is dropped in water?
Draw pictures to help you to explain.
Use ○ for a water particle.
Use ● for an aspirin particle.

3　This coffee filter collects the coffee
grains. Why does the water pass
through the filter paper?

4　To make a balloon lighter than air
you could fill it with a light gas.
Hydrogen is a light gas.
a)　Why isn't hydrogen used to fill
passenger balloons?
b)　Find out all you can about the
Hindenburg.

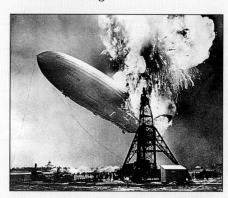

Things to do

95

Particles on the move

Learn about:
- using particle theory to explain results and observations

▶ Draw 3 diagrams to show how you think particles are arranged in a solid, a liquid and a gas.

How do your diagrams explain that:

a solids are hard to compress (squash)?
b gases are easy to compress?
c liquids can be poured?
d gases are the shape of their container?

We know that materials **expand** when they get hot.
They **contract** when they cool down.

e What does *expand* mean?
f What does *contract* mean?
g When a solid expands, what do you think happens to the particles?

▶ Look at your answers to **e**, **f** and **g**.
Use these to help you with the photo questions.

j Boiling water should not be poured into a cold glass. Why not?

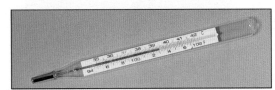

h Why is mercury used in thermometers?

i Railway tracks contain small gaps. Why do they have these?

k Concrete roads have gaps between sections. Why are these filled with tar?

l Warming the jam jar lid may help to remove it. Why?

Watching for movement

Do particles move? Try some of these tests to find out.

A blue move?
Before you do this test, predict what will happen.

Put a few blue crystals in the bottom of a beaker.
Carefully pour water on the top.
Do not shake or stir.
Leave the beaker for a few days.
Draw pictures to show what happens.

Use some of these words to explain what happens.

dissolve   move
particles   spread
blue   mix
water   collide

Do you think particles move?
Write down or draw what you think happens to the particles.

Smoke signals?

Your teacher will show you this experiment.

When fumes from the acid and ammonia meet, white smoke forms.

What do you think will happen in this experiment?
Predict *exactly* what you will see.

Your teacher will do this experiment.
Try to explain what you see.

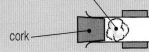

cotton wool soaked in concentrated ammonia solution

cotton wool soaked in concentrated hydrochloric acid

cork

A brown move?

Your teacher will show you the bromine experiment.

What happens when a gas jar of air is put on top of a gas jar of bromine?
Do you think the particles move?
Write down or draw what you think happens to the particles.

air

bromine in gas jar

Diffusion

Liquid and gas particles can move and mix. They do this without being stirred or shaken. This is called **diffusion**.

Have you ever smelt freshly baked bread?
Particles of gas are released from the bread. They **diffuse** through the air. You can smell the bread throughout the room.

The ***Watching for movement*** tests tell you about *rates* of diffusion too.

m Which diffuses faster, a gas or a liquid? Why?

---

1 Copy and complete:

a) 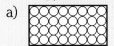 These are the particles in a . . . .

b) 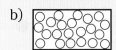 These are the particles in a . . . .

c) 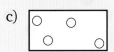 These are the particles in a . . . .

2 Robert Brown was a Scottish scientist. He studied pollen grains in water. Find out about what he saw. This is called Brownian motion.

3 Helium is a lighter gas than air.
Gas particles can diffuse through balloon rubber. This is why balloons go down.

Which balloon do you think will go down first? Why?

Things to do

Diffusing

Learn about:
● the movement of particles
● diffusion
● using models

What did you decide about particles? Can they move?
Scientists think that particles move.

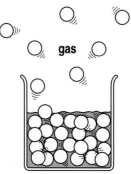
gas

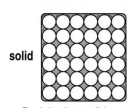
solid

Particles in a solid are close together. They do not move about but they do vibrate.

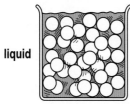
liquid

Particles in a liquid move about. They are still close together.

Particles in a gas move about quickly. They move in all directions. They are further away from each other.

▶ Look at these pictures. They all give clues about gas particles moving.

picture 1

A lovely smell.

picture 2

PETROLEUM SPIRIT HIGHLY FLAMMABLE

NO SMOKING

picture 3

TANKER CRASH LATEST

The tanker was carrying ammonia. The gas can affect eyes and breathing. People living within a 3 mile radius of the crash were moved from their homes.

picture 4

The pictures tell you that gas particles can move and mix.
They do this without being stirred or shaken.
Remember that this is called **diffusion**.

a Write about 2 lines to say what is happening to the gas particles in picture 1.

b The roses in picture 2 smell lovely. Draw them and show how their smell spreads in a room. Use dots to represent particles. (Hint: lots of dots together mean a strong smell.)

c Why is 'No smoking' important at the petrol station in picture 3?

d Look at picture 4. Why did people living 3 miles from the crash have to be moved?

e Think of some tests you could carry out to see if *solids* diffuse. Write down:
  ● what you would do
  ● how you would know about any diffusion.

Predict the results of your tests.
Explain your prediction using ideas about particles.

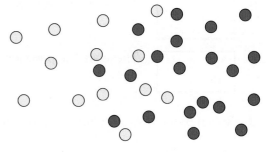

No confusion – it's **diffusion**

Early ideas about particles

The first people to think that matter is made up of tiny particles were the ancient Greeks. The idea was developed by Democritus who was born in 460BC. He was a wealthy philosopher. He used the ideas of his teacher to explain his observations of the world.

Democritus

> I believe that everything is made of particles.
> The particles are so small we can't see them. They can't be destroyed and they are really hard.

> So how come we have lots of different materials — like water and iron — if they are all made of particles?

> Well each material must be made up of different particles. For example, water can flow, so its particles must be smooth and round. However, iron is hard and strong — its particles must be strong and jagged. They get jammed in place next to each other.

The ideas of Democritus could explain lots of things. He had constructed a good **model**. However, many centuries later our theories about particles changed as scientists found out more about chemical reactions.

And they are still changing today as new observations are made with the help of modern technology.

Ideas about particles

What have you learnt about particles in this topic ?
Make a patterned note to show your ideas.
Try to include these words:

solid	liquid	gas	expand
diffuse	melt	move	vibrate
contract	mix	spread	Democritus

1 Describe the differences in the way particles move in a solid, a liquid and a gas.

2 Draw a particle picture to show ink and water diffusing.
Use coloured dots to represent particles.

3 Describe in your own words what all particles have in common according to Democritus.

4 In what ways does Democritus say that one type of particle differs from another?

5 Using the ideas of Democritus:
a) Draw the particles in water.
b) Draw the particles in a piece of iron.

6 In what ways do your ideas about particles differ from those of Democritus?

7 Find out about other ancient Greeks who contributed towards scientific thinking at that time.
Write about their ideas and anything you can find out about their lives.

Things to do

Gases and pressure

Learn about:
- particles in a gas
- what causes gas pressure

▶ Copy out each label. Say whether it is for a **solid**, a **liquid** or a **gas**. (Clue: there are 2 labels for each!)

The particles are very close together. They are in a regular pattern.

The particles move about quickly and in all directions.

The particles are far apart and arranged randomly.

The particles do not move about. They vibrate.

The particles are close together but randomly arranged.

The particles move about.

▶ Look at the 2 labels you have chosen for gases. These tell you about **gas pressure**.

Gas pressure . . .

. . . keeps a balloon blown up.

. . . tells us about the weather.

. . . gives us a comfy bike ride!

Gas pressure

What causes the pressure? Particles help us to understand.
Think about gas inside a balloon.
The particles move around very quickly.
They move in all directions. Some particles hit each other.
Others hit the wall of the balloon. Those that hit the wall give a force on each unit of area of the balloon. This is called the **pressure** of the gas.

The *more often* particles hit the wall, the *greater* the pressure.
The *harder* they hit the wall, the *greater* the pressure.

Think about gases

Make some predictions. Discuss these in your group.

1. Think of a gas in a closed box. What happens if you heat the gas? Do you think the pressure will increase or decrease? Try to explain using the idea of particles.

2. Think of a gas in a syringe. The plunger can move in and out. What happens to the plunger if you heat the gas? Try to explain using the idea of particles.

Check your predictions with your teacher.

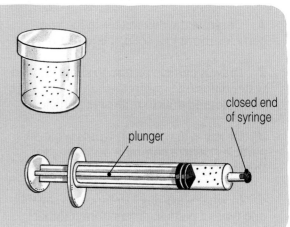

closed end of syringe

plunger

Moving gases

Your teacher will show you an experiment using a porous pot.
The porous pot lets gas particles through its walls.
Your teacher will put some natural gas into the beaker.
The gas is lighter than air.
Think about the movement of gas particles.

Try to explain what you see.
Use your ideas about gas pressure and diffusion.

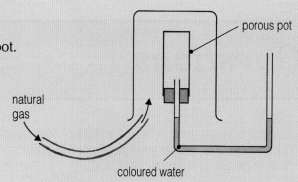

porous pot

natural gas

coloured water

Gases into liquids

Gases can be turned into liquids. One way to do this is to put the gas in a pressurised container. We say the gas is **compressed** or stored **under pressure**.

a Why does *compressing* a gas turn it to a liquid?
Use particles to explain.

You have probably seen tankers like the one in the photograph:
This one is used to carry liquid nitrogen.

b Why are gases stored and transported as liquids?

Liquid nitrogen is very useful. It is very cold.
Lots of foods are frozen by spraying them with liquid nitrogen.

c Why do we freeze foods?

d Are frozen foods good for you? Write about your ideas.

Propane and butane can also be stored as liquids.

e What are these gases used for?

f What are the dangers of these gases?

g Why does the pressure in a butane cylinder fall when the temperature falls?

---

1 Copy and complete:
Particles in a gas . . . . quickly in . . . .
directions. When they hit the . . . . of a
container this is called the gas . . . . This is
the . . . . on each unit of area. Gas particles
move more . . . . when they are heated. As
the gas is heated in the container, the
pressure . . . .

2

PIZAZ
SPORT

WARNING Contains flammable solvents.
Pressurised container: protect from sunlight and do not expose to temperatures
exceeding 50°C. Do not pierce or burn,
even after use. Do not spray on a naked
flame or any incandescent material.
Ensure adequate ventilation when in use.
Keep out of reach of children.

Why shouldn't you put this near to heat?

3 Look at these boiling points of gases that are in the air.

xenon	−108°C	krypton	−153°C
argon	−186°C	nitrogen	−196°C
oxygen	−183°C	helium	−269°C
	neon	−246°C	

To collect the gases, air is cooled so it becomes liquid. The liquid air is slowly warmed so the gases boil off.
a) Which 2 gases have the closest boiling points?
b) When liquid air is warmed, which boils off first – oxygen, argon or nitrogen?
c) What is this method of separating called?
d) Which gas is the most common in the air?
e) Which gas is needed for burning?
f) Name another gas found in the air. (Clue: breathe out!)

Things to do

Questions

1   Imagine you are the teacher of a class of 10-year-olds.
    Think about some tests your pupils could do to
    classify things as solids or liquids.

    Design a worksheet which shows:
    • the apparatus pupils need
    • clear instructions for each test
    • the results expected for solids
    • the results expected for liquids.

    Make sure your worksheet is interesting!
    You could draw diagrams, cartoons or pictures on it.
    You could even set some homework!

GRAND HIGH SCHOOL
What is a solid?

Tests for you:

2   Choose one of the gases you know about.
    Design a poster for 10-year-old children to tell them about
    this gas and its uses.

3   Plan an investigation to find out how much gas is given
    off by one can of fizzy drink.

4   Explain each of the following statements.
    a) Heating a metal top on a glass jar helps
        you to remove the top.
    b) The Eiffel Tower is smaller in winter
        than in summer.
    c) Icing on a cake can run.

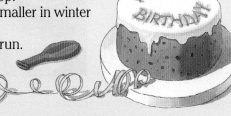

5   A purple crystal is put into a beaker of water.
    It starts to dissolve.
    Draw pictures to show what you think will be seen:
    a) after 10 minutes   b) after 2 hours   c) after 2 weeks.

6   Look at the diagram opposite:

    a) Explain how this apparatus could be used as a simple thermometer.
    b) What happens to the water particles as the temperature rises?
    c) Could you use this to measure the temperature of boiling oil?
        Explain your answer.
    d) Could you use this to measure the temperature inside a freezer?
        Explain your answer.

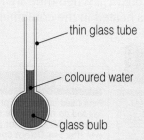

thin glass tube

coloured water

glass bulb

7   What makes a good group discussion?
    In this topic you have discussed lots of ideas and problems.
    Draw up a set of points to look for, which your teacher could use to
    judge how well you discuss.

Solutions

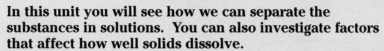

Do you enjoy a cup of tea or a glass of orange squash?
We are all used to making solutions and drinking them!

In this unit you will see how we can separate the
substances in solutions. You can also investigate factors
that affect how well solids dissolve.

Any solution?

Penny, Mike and Chung were talking about **dissolving** things.

Who do you think was right?

"No, that's called melting."

"...Perhaps melting and dissolving are the same thing."

"It's when a solid turns to a liquid."

▶ Imagine you are the pupils' teacher.

Try to help this group understand melting and dissolving.

Write down what you would say to each person.

Making a solution

In this experiment you can test some solids to see if they dissolve in water.

- Half fill a test-tube with water.

- Add 1 spatula measure of solid to the water.

- Shake the tube gently for 1 minute.

- Look to see if any of the solid has disappeared. If so, it must have **dissolved**.

- Do the experiment again with other solids.

Adding the solid   Checking the solution

Solids which dissolve are said to be **soluble**.

Solids which do not dissolve are said to be **insoluble**.

a Which solids are soluble in water?

b Which solids are insoluble in water?

c Penny says "You can use this experiment to see which substance is the most soluble."
Is she right?
Give Penny some advice on how she could improve the experiment.

"I've still got some solid left. Is there less than at the start?"

Sometimes it is hard to tell if a solid has dissolved.

d How could you test to see if any solid has dissolved?

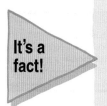

Think about dissolving

Hypotheses are ideas about things which always happen (see page 178).

You can make a hypothesis.
From this you can make a **prediction**.
Then you can collect evidence to see if it is true.

Mike had a hypothesis about dissolving.
He said "I think substances always dissolve faster if they are stirred."
Do you think he was right?

Think about **your own** work on dissolving.
Write down your own hypothesis about dissolving.
Use your ideas about particles to predict what will happen.

Plan an investigation to test your prediction.

How can you make your results reliable?

Ask your teacher if you can carry out your investigation.

(see page 178)

Things to do

1 Copy and complete:
a) Solids which dissolve are called . . . . solids.
b) . . . . solids do not dissolve.
c) A solid is said to dissolve if it . . . . when put in water.

2 Plan an investigation to test Mike's idea about dissolving.

3 Draw particle diagrams to show what you think happens when:
a) a solid melts
b) a solid dissolves in water.

4 a) How do you know a liquid is *pure*? What tests could you do to find out? Describe your tests.
The words in the box may give you some ideas:

> filter   thermometer
> boil   evaporate

b) Is sea-water the same as pure water? Explain your answer.

Rock salt

Learn about:
● getting pure salt from rock salt
● uses of salt

Do you like salt on your food?
Do you know where the salt comes from?
How is it extracted to use on food?
Your work on solutions may help you to answer these questions!

▶ Look at the photographs opposite:

They show samples of salt.

What is happening in each one?
Write down your ideas.

The chemical name for salt is sodium chloride.
It is found in sea-water and in rock salt.
In hot countries the salt is extracted from sea-water. Heat from the Sun **evaporates** the water. It changes the water from liquid to gas.
The solid salt gets left behind.

a Why don't we get much salt this way in Britain?

In Britain we can get salt from rock salt.
The rock salt is found about 300 m below ground.
It is a mixture of salt and bits of rock.
How could you get **pure** salt from this rock salt?

Rock salt

Getting pure salt

Look at the diagrams below. They show how to get pure salt from rock salt.

Step 1

b What are the mortar and pestle used for?

pestle   mortar
rock salt

Step 2

The salt dissolves.
It is soluble.

c What happens to the pieces of rock and sand?

rock salt
glass rod
water

Step 3

The mixture is filtered.

d What is in the evaporating basin?

e What is left in the filter paper?

Step 4

The water evaporates.

f What is left in the basin?

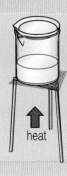
heat

How much salt?

Use the diagrams on page 106 to help you with this.
Choose **one** of these experiments to plan.

$$\text{percentage of pure salt} = \frac{\text{mass of pure salt}}{\text{mass of rock salt}} \times 100\%$$

Plan an experiment:

- to get some pure salt from rock salt

or

- to find out the percentage of pure salt in a sample of rock salt

or

- to compare the salt content of two different samples of rock salt.

Explain carefully what you will do. Have your plan checked by your teacher before you start the experiment.

Did your plan work? Would you do anything different next time?

Salt is a very important substance.

▶ Look at some of its uses:

Uses of salt

It is used on roads in winter. It lowers the freezing point of water.

To make sodium. This gives the yellow glow in street lights

To make sodium hydroxide. This is used to make soap.

To make chlorine. This is used in bleach.

It flavours food.

Things to do

1 Copy and complete:
a) Rock salt is a . . . . of salt and bits of rock.
b) Pure salt can be made by . . . . the rock salt, then adding water to . . . . the pure salt, filtering to remove the . . . . and heating the salt . . . . to evaporate the water.
c) Rock salt is spread on roads in winter. It helps to . . . . the snow and ice.

2 Lucy got some pure salt from her rock salt.
Why was the mass of the pure salt less than the mass of the rock salt she started with?

3 Supermarkets sell 'low sodium' salt.
a) How is this different to normal salt?
b) Why do some people choose to buy it?

4 Salt has had many uses over the years.
Try to find out what it was used for in the past.
Draw or write about your findings.

Dissolved particles

Do you drink tea or coffee? If you do, do you add sugar?
You can find out more about sugar dissolving on this page.

Where has it gone?

When some solids are put into a liquid like water, they appear to get smaller. Some solids seem to disappear. Remember that if the solid looks like it disappears, we say it has **dissolved**.

a What do we call the liquid we get when a solid dissolves?

▶ Think about particles on the move.
Discuss these questions in your group.

● Why does sugar dissolve when you put it into a cup of tea?

● Where do the sugar particles go?

● Does the sugar dissolve faster in cold tea or hot tea?

● Do sugar particles move faster in cold tea or hot tea?

Investigating solutions

1. Jawad was investigating solutions.

   He filled a beaker to the 200 cm³ mark with water.
   He then used a balance to find the mass of beaker + water.

   Mass of beaker + water = __ g

   He added sugar granules to the water. He stirred the water until he could not see the sugar. It had dissolved.
   He used the balance to find the mass of beaker + sugar solution.

   Mass of beaker + sugar solution = __ g

b Predict Jawad's results:
do you think the mass will stay the same? … get smaller? … get bigger?

c Why did you choose this answer?

Now try Jawad's experiment for yourself.

d What do you find?

2. In his next experiment, Jawad measured the mass of the beaker, the water in it and some solid sugar.
   The mass was 210 g.
   Then he added the sugar to the water and stirred it.

e What do you think Jawad found out?

Predict the mass of the beaker and sugar solution.

Now try Jawad's experiment for yourself.

f What do you find?

Applying the particle theory

So what happens to the particles in sugar when they dissolve in water?

Look at the model below:

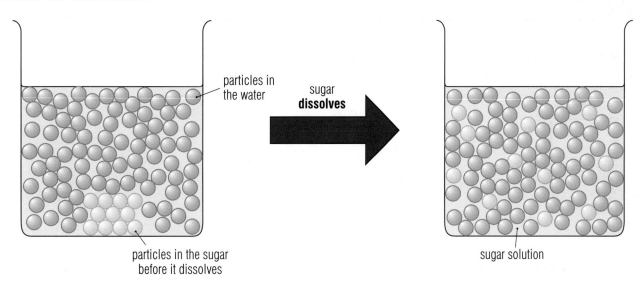

particles in the water

sugar **dissolves**

particles in the sugar before it dissolves

sugar solution

The particles in the water are 'attracted' to the particles in the sugar. We can think of the particles in the sugar being 'dragged away' from each other.
They become surrounded by particles of water.
Water is a liquid.
The particles in the water are moving around.
This movement makes sure that the particles of sugar get spread throughout the solution formed.

g Why do you think we stir a cup of tea with sugar in it?

Look at the photo of granulated sugar and sugar cubes:

h Which of these dissolves faster?
Explain why.

---

1 Match each of the following descriptions with the correct word.

	Description	Word
a)	solid seeming to disappear in a liquid	diffusing
b)	particles moving and mixing	predicting
c)	the liquid made when a solid dissolves	mass
d)	saying what you think will happen	solution
e)	a measurement made in grams	dissolving

2 Look at the contents of the cupboards in your kitchen.
Do any of the labels or containers talk about dissolving?
Make a note of what is said.

Product	Notes on dissolving
oven cleaner	dissolves grease and baked on food

3 Think about dissolving a sugar cube in water. Imagine that you are one of the sugar particles. Describe what happens to you as you dissolve.

Things to do

More dissolving

Learn about:
● particles and dissolving
● solvents other than water

There's a lot of science in action when you make tea.

▶ Look at what you do:

Boiling the water.

Brewing the tea.

Adding milk and sugar.

Write about the particles in each step shown above.
Where are they? What is happening to them?
Start with the water particles in the kettle. Finish with the particles
in your cup of milky sweet tea.
Try to use some or all of these words and phrases:

moving slowly	*moving more quickly*	*steam*	*diffuse*	*soluble*
insoluble	*close together*	*far apart*	*dissolve*	*mix*

Sugar dissolves in a hot cup of tea. It dissolves in the water.
It makes a **solution**. Sugar is **soluble**.
In a solution the substance which dissolves is the **solute**. Sugar is the **solute**.
The water dissolves the sugar.
The water is the **solvent**.

solute	+	**solvent**	⟶	**solution**

Dissolving quickly

Think about all the things that affect dissolving.
How could you get a sugar cube to dissolve as
quickly as possible?

a Make a list of your
ideas.

b Explain each idea
in terms of particles.

Making a solution

Emma adds the salt to the water
in the beaker.

c When all the salt has
dissolved, what is the
reading on the balance?
Explain this using the
idea of particles.

d How can Emma get
the solid salt back?

5.5 g of salt

water

In most solutions the solvent is water. But other substances can be solvents

Have you ever had any clothes dry-cleaned?
Dry cleaning uses solvents without water in them.
These are called non-aqueous solvents.

e What type of stains can dry-cleaning remove?

f Why don't we dry-clean **all** our clothes?

Nail varnish remover is another non-aqueous solvent.

g What is its chemical name?

MADE IN RUSSIA
57% VISCOSE/Вискоза
43% ACETATE/Ацетат
LINING/Подкладка
100% POLYESTER/
Полизфир

M20627

PROFESSIONAL
DRY CLEAN
ONLY

Clean nails

Paint some nail varnish on a glass slide.
Leave it to dry for a few minutes.
Test the 3 solvents your teacher will give you.
Which is best at removing the varnish?

Some solutes are very soluble in a solvent but they may be **in**soluble in another solvent.
They have different **solubilities** in different solvents.

A stain remover

Plan an investigation on solvents.
Which solvent is best at removing stains?

Your teacher will give you some substances which stain.
Examples could be:

ball-point pen   felt-tip pen   grease

paint   grass   coffee   tea

orange juice   tomato sauce

Ask your teacher to check your plan.
Then do the investigation.

⚠ Some solvents are very flammable.
Make sure there are no Bunsens
alight in the lab.

1 Copy and complete:
a) A substance which .... is soluble.
b) A substance which does not .... is insoluble.
c) solute + solvent → ....
d) Solvents without .... are non-aqueous.
e) Solutes have different .... in different solvents.

2 Which of these are soluble in water?
a) sand
b) salt
c) chalk
d) butter
e) wax
f) sugar
g) detergent

3 Sea-water is a solution. Name a solute and the solvent in sea-water.

4 What's the difference between these felt-tip pens?

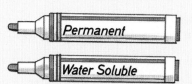

Permanent

Water Soluble

5 Design an investigation to show how the temperature of the water affects the speed at which a solid dissolves in it.
Draw a diagram of the apparatus you would use.

Things to do

Separating mixtures

Learn about:
● distillation
● chromatography
● working out how to separate mixtures

You have seen what happens to particles when we make a solution. Do you think we could separate and collect the solvent from a solution? How?

Distilling solutions

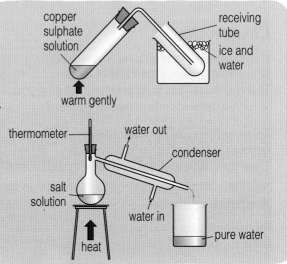

copper sulphate solution
receiving tube
ice and water
warm gently

Try the experiment shown opposite:

a What do you see collecting in your receiving tube?

b Try to explain what is happening to the copper sulphate solution.

We can collect the solvent more effectively using a **condenser**.

Look at the apparatus for carrying out a simple **distillation**:

thermometer
water out
condenser
salt solution
water in
heat
pure water

c How do you think the condenser works?

d Explain what happens to the particles in the salt and water during distillation.

Separating dyes

In this experiment you will use **chromatography** to separate dyes in inks. Inks are often a mixture of dyes. You can try this with felt-tip pen or pen inks.

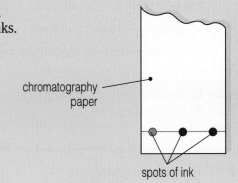

chromatography paper

spots of ink

● Cut a piece of chromatography paper to fit inside a beaker. Draw a faint pencil line about 1 cm above the bottom of the paper.

● Carefully use a felt-tip pen or a teat-pipette to spot some ink on the line. Put the spot about 1 cm away from the edge. Make the spot about 2 or 3 mm in diameter.

● Leaving 1 cm spaces, put spots of other inks on the line.

● Carefully put about 0.5 cm depth of water in your beaker. Try not to wet the sides of the beaker.

● Now put your chromatography paper in the beaker as shown in the diagram. Wrap the top of the paper round a pencil to keep it upright in the water.

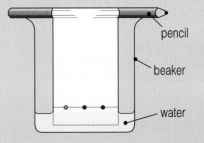

pencil
beaker
water

● Let the water soak up the paper. Take the paper out when the water is nearly at the top of the paper.

e Why must the ink spots be above the level of water at the start?

f Why do you think the different dyes separate during chromatography? Refer to 'particles' in your answer.

g How could you improve this experiment to get a better separation?

Make a table to show your results:

Colour of ink	Number of dyes in ink	Colour of dyes in ink

Separating mixtures

Think about the following mixtures. Discuss them in your group.
Say what experiments you would do to separate the parts of
the mixture in each case.

Think about the safety of your experiments.
What are the dangers?
What precautions should you take?

Ask your teacher for a Help Sheet if you get stuck!

Mixture 1 – Mud in the garden!
Get dry soil from the water.

Mixture 2 – Swimming makes you thirsty!
Get pure water from sea-water.

Mixture 3 – A broken sugar bowl!
Get the pieces of glass from the sugar.

Mixture 4 – Colours unmixed!
Get the red dye from the purple mixture.

Your teacher may let you try some of these experiments.

For each of your separations:

- Draw a flow-chart to show what you did.
- Say whether your experiment was successful.
- Describe one way you could improve the experiment next time.
- Use particle ideas to explain how your experiments work.

---

1 a) Draw the apparatus you could use to separate the water from blue ink.
b) Draw the particles in blue ink and explain what happens to them in the apparatus from part a).

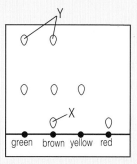

2 Look at the properties of A, B and C.
How would you separate a mixture of them?

Substance	Dissolves in cold water?	Dissolves in hot water?
A	✗	✓
B	✗	✗
C	✓	✓

3 Why can we use this to strain tea but not coffee?

4 Chromatography can show which dyes are in different coloured inks.

green brown yellow red

a) Which 2 inks contain only one dye?
b) Which ink contains 3 dyes?
c) Which colour would the spot X be?
d) Predict which colour the spots labelled Y would be.

Things to do

Make it saturated

Learn about:
- saturated solutions
- making and interpreting solubility curves

▶ Nazia makes a solution from 4 g of salt and 100 g of water. Describe 2 ways she could make a solution which is *half* as concentrated.

Some solutions contain only *a little solute* in *a lot of solvent*. We say the solutions are **dilute**.
Some solutions contain *a lot of solute* in only *a little solvent*. We say the solutions are **concentrated**.

What happens if we heat a concentrated solution?

As more and more solvent evaporates, the solution becomes more and more concentrated.
Eventually it cannot become any more concentrated.
If more solvent evaporates, solute comes out of the solution.
We see solid forming. The solution is **saturated**.

A **saturated** solution is one in which no more solute will dissolve (at that temperature).

Which orange drink is more concentrated?

Plotting solubility curves

The amount of a substance that can dissolve in a certain amount of solvent (at that temperature) is called the **solubility** of the substance.

We can measure the solubility of a substance at different temperatures. If the information is plotted on a graph, it makes a **solubility curve**.

Different amounts of copper sulphate dissolve at different temperatures

▶ Use the information in the table to plot a solubility curve for potassium chloride:

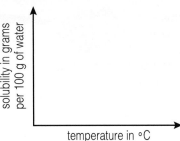

a   What is the solubility of potassium chloride at 45°C?

b   At what temperature does 36 g of potassium chloride dissolve in 100 g of water?

c   At 80°C, how much potassium chloride dissolves in 1 kg (1000 g) of water?

d   At 40°C, how much potassium chloride dissolves in 50 g of water?

e   At 25°C, how much potassium chloride dissolves in 20 g of water?

f   What happens to the solubility of potassium chloride as the temperature increases?

Temperature in °C	Solubility in grams per 100 g of water
0	28.0
10	31.0
20	34.5
30	37.5
40	40.0
50	43.0
60	45.5
70	48.5
80	51.0
90	54.0
100	56.5

This table shows how the solubility of potassium chloride changes with temperature

In hot countries you can get salt from sea-water.
As the water evaporates, the salt solution becomes **saturated**.
This means that the solid salt appears.
It crystallises and is collected.

Testing solubility

Plan a test to see which substance is the most soluble in water.

Think about:

- How will you make this a fair test**?**
- How will you make your solutions saturated**?**
- How will you measure how much solid dissolves**?**
- How will you make your results reliable**?**
- What apparatus will you use**?**
- How will you record your results**?**

Ask your teacher to check your plan.
You can then collect some substances to test.

Which is the most soluble**?**

1 Explain the meanings of each of these
words or phrases:
a) solution
b) saturated solution
c) solubility
d) solubility curve.

2 At 60°C, 40 g of copper sulphate
dissolves in 100 g of water to make a
saturated solution.
a) At 60°C, how much will dissolve in 250 g
of water?
b) At 60°C, how much will dissolve in 46 g
of water?
c) Why is the solubility of solids in water
normally given only for temperatures
between 0°C–100°C?

3 A hot, saturated solution of
potassium nitrate in water is cooled to room
temperature. Describe what you would see.
(Use the graph for question 4 to help you.)

4 Look at these solubility curves:

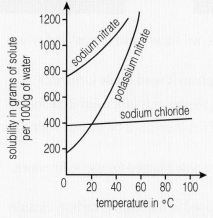

a) Which substance is the most soluble at
room temperature?
b) Which substance is the least soluble at
room temperature? (Explain your
answer carefully!)
c) Which substance has a solubility which
changes only a little with temperature?

Things to do

Chemistry at Work

A **foam** is a mixture of a solid or a liquid with gas trapped inside it.
We see many foams in everyday life.
Look at the photos below:

A

B

C

D

E

F

G

a Which of the photos above show 'solid foams' and which show 'liquid foams'?

b Why is the mixture in photo A used inside furniture?

c How do you think that the gas gets inside furniture foam?

d All foam used to make furniture must be treated with a flame retardant. Why?

e Some types of foam are now banned for use in furniture. Explain why.

f In photo B, the gas trapped in the foam is carbon dioxide. Carbon dioxide extinguishes a flame. Why is the foam used?

g What is the liquid that you beat with a whisk when you make meringue?

h Why is the liquid in **g** beaten with a whisk to make meringue?

Emulsions are mixtures of liquids that don't really mix well together! The liquids are **immiscible**. They form layers.
For example, when oil and water are shaken up they form an emulsion. Emulsifying agents are added to foods to stop the oily liquids separating from the watery solutions.

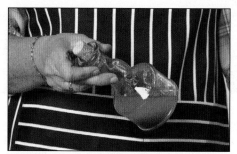

Emulsifying agents are used in salad dressing

i   Carry out a survey of some food labels to identify which foods contain emulsifying agents.

j   Where would you use an emulsion when decorating your house?

k   Find out how the oil and water stay mixed in salad cream.

Uses of chromatography

Scientists can separate and identify mixtures of solutes when given a solution.

They can compare their chromatograms with those from known substances. The results of chromatograms are collected in databases or books of data.
The technique is used to identify small traces of substances.

For example, chromatography is used to test for drugs in horse racing. It can also be used in hospitals to analyse the substances in urine. Forensic scientists use chromatography to help solve crimes.

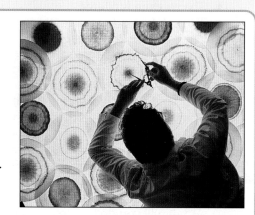

Look at the example of a chromatogram from a new fruit drink below. The food scientist is checking whether or not the drink contains a banned dye:

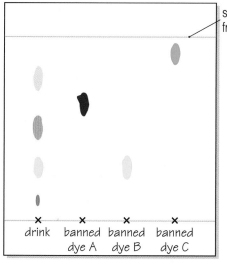

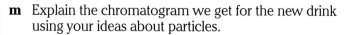
drink   banned   banned   banned
         dye A   dye B   dye C

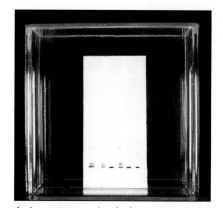

A chromatogram developing

l   Imagine you are the food scientist. Write a report of your findings.

m   Explain the chromatogram we get for the new drink using your ideas about particles.

Questions

1 The 9 sentences below are about the process for getting pure salt from rock salt. Put the sentences in the right order so that the information makes sense.
Copy out the sentences when you have the right order.

A sample of rock salt

- Rock salt is crushed into small pieces.
- The mixture is filtered.
- The solution is heated gently.
- The pure salt dissolves.
- The mixture is warmed and stirred.
- The salt solution passes through the filter paper.
- Water is added to the mixture.
- The sand and dirt collect in the filter paper.
- The water evaporates to leave dry salt.

2 You have been asked to make a jelly for your brother's birthday party. The party is due to start in 2 hours!

a) What will you do to dissolve the jelly cubes in water as quickly as possible?
b) Explain what happens to the particles in the jelly as it dissolves.
c) Look at the things you listed in part a). How does each one affect how quickly the jelly dissolves? Use particle theory in your answer.

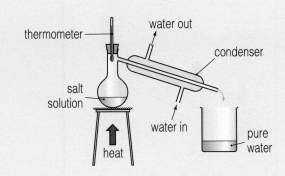

3 Look at the apparatus opposite:

a) What do we call this technique?
b) What temperature will the thermometer read as water is being collected?
c) Explain how the technique works.
d) How could you separate the dyes in food colouring?

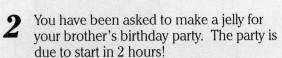

4 You have a solution of potassium nitrate in water. The solution is saturated.
How can you find out the solubility of potassium nitrate at room temperature?
What apparatus will you need? Describe what you will do.
What measurements will you make?
Show how you will calculate the solubility.

Energy resources

7I

Without energy nothing can ever happen!

All living things need energy to stay alive and to move.
You get your energy from your food.

Machines cannot work without energy.
Our homes, transport and factories need the energy that
comes from fuels.

119

What is energy?

7I1

Learn about:
- transferring energy
- energy transfer diagrams
- measuring energy in joules

We often use the word '**energy**'.
Tina says, "I've got lots of energy today."
John says, "I haven't got enough energy to climb the hill."
A car driver says, "I need some more petrol – my car has almost run out of energy."

▶ Write down three sentences of your own, using the word 'energy'.

▶ What do you think the word 'energy' means?
Where do you get your energy from?

▶ Look at the photograph. How many examples of energy can you find? Make a list.

Energy diagrams

Energy is needed to get jobs done, or make things work.
To get a job done, energy must be moved or **transferred** from one place to another.

Example 1

Suppose you wind up a clockwork toy, and then let it run across the table.
Where are the energy transfers?

start
energy stored in your body → energy stored in the wound-up spring → movement energy of the toy

This is an **Energy Transfer Diagram**.

Example 2

Sometimes an Energy Transfer Diagram splits into two or more parts.
Suppose you switch on a torch:

energy stored in the battery → energy lighting up the room

energy heating up the bulb

The energy heating up the bulb is **wasted** energy. It is not useful.

Example 3

Rub your hands together quickly about 20 times.
What do you notice? Copy and complete this energy diagram:

. . . . stored in my . . . . → movement energy of my hands → energy . . . . up my hands

. . . . of the sound made by my hands

Energy transfers

Try each of these experiments and observe them carefully.
Think about the energy transfers. For each one:
- sketch a diagram of the equipment, and
- draw an Energy Transfer Diagram.

a a clockwork car

b a battery and a lamp bulb

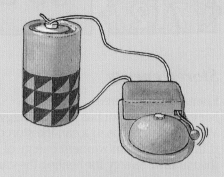

c a battery and a buzzer or door-bell

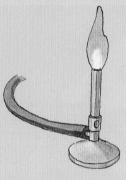

d a Bunsen burner

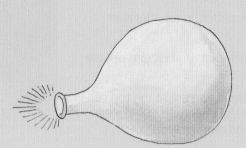

e blow up a balloon and then release it

f a dynamo and a lamp

Measuring energy

Sometimes we need to measure the amount of energy. The unit we use for measuring energy is the **joule**. This is written as **J** for short.

The joule is named after James Joule (1818–1889) who did many experiments on energy.

A joule is a small unit of energy. To lift an apple from the floor up on to a table needs about 1 joule of energy.

But if you *eat* the apple, it will give you a lot of energy – about 200 000 joules of energy. That's enough energy to walk up 50 flights of stairs!

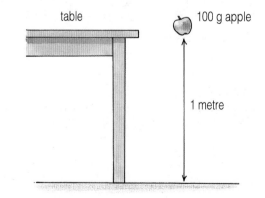

table   100 g apple

1 metre

---

1 Copy and complete:
a) . . . . is needed to get jobs done.
b) Energy is measured in . . . .

2 Draw a diagram to show the energy transfers when you pedal a bicycle.
Label it clearly.
How do you think it will change if you oil your bike?

3 Draw an Energy Transfer Diagram for a battery-powered television set.

4 Draw Energy Transfer Diagrams for:
a) a girl firing an arrow from a bow
b) a boy kicking a football
c) a bonfire burning
d) a firework rocket
e) a petrol-powered car.

Things to do

Go with energy

Learn about:
- forms of energy
- the energy law

Stored energy

Energy can be stored.
For example, petrol has stored energy.
When petrol burns in a car, the stored energy
is transferred to movement energy of
the car **and** energy for heating the car:

Stored energy is often called **potential energy**.

petrol in a car

energy heating up
the car and the air

potential energy
stored in petrol

movement energy
of the car

Here are some examples of stored energy:

- **Chemical energy**   For example: in petrol; in a battery; in
  the food that you eat.

- **Strain energy**   For example: in a catapult; in a clockwork car;
  in a balloon that has been blown up.

- **Gravitational energy**   For example: if you are at the top of
  a ladder, you have gravitational potential energy.
  If you fall off the ladder, the energy will damage you!

- Look at the photograph. What energy does the skier have at
  the top of the hill?

  When she skis down, this potential energy is transferred to her
  movement energy. (Another name for movement energy is
  kinetic energy.)

▶ Look back at experiments **a–f** on page 121.
  Where is the stored energy in each one? Make a list.

potential energy ➡ kinetic energy

The energy law

Here is an energy diagram for a battery
connected to an electric motor:

If we measure the amount of energy (in
joules) **before** the transfer and **after** the
transfer, we find **it is the same amount**.

In the diagram, 100 joules of energy stored
in the battery is transferred to 70 joules of
movement energy and 30 joules of energy
heating up the motor.
So: 100 = 70 + 30,   the same amount of energy.

model racing car

100 J
potential energy
stored in the
battery

70 J
movement
energy

30 J
energy heating
up the motor
(wasted energy)

However, only 70 joules of energy are useful to us, as movement
energy. The other 30 J are wasted, because they are no use to us.

This is what usually happens in energy transfers.
**Although there is the same amount of energy afterwards,
not all of it is useful.**

A steam engine

Look carefully at a steam engine doing a job of work.

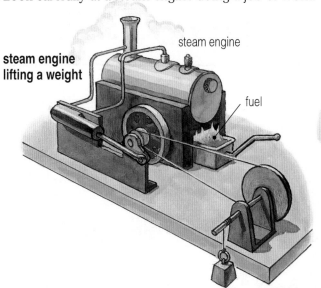

steam engine lifting a weight

steam engine

fuel

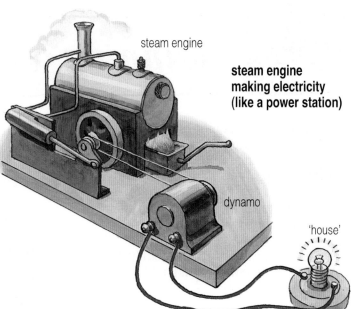

steam engine

steam engine making electricity (like a power station)

dynamo

'house'

▶ Observe each one carefully and look for energy transfers.
Draw an Energy Transfer Diagram for each one. Try to include all of the energy changes.

Investigating a clockwork toy

Plan an investigation to see how the **distance travelled** by a clockwork toy depends on **how much it is wound up**.

- How will you measure the distance accurately?
- Will you wind it up in full-turn steps or half-turn steps?
- How will you ensure it is a **fair test**?
- How can you make your results more reliable?

Ask your teacher to check your plan. How can you improve it?

Things to do

1 Copy and complete:
a) Stored energy is also called . . . . energy.
b) This includes chemical . . . . , ... energy and . . . . energy.
c) An Energy . . . . Diagram shows us how the energy is . . . .
d) The amount of . . . . before the transfer is always . . . . to the amount of energy . . . . the transfer.

2 A battery is connected to a lamp bulb. Draw an Energy Transfer Diagram for this. While it is switched on, the battery gives out 100 joules of energy. If 80 J are heating up the room, how many joules are lighting the room?

3 Which of these two words could you use for each of these examples – **potential** (stored) energy or **kinetic** (movement) energy:
a) a can of petrol?
b) a car travelling down a road?
c) water at the very top of a waterfall?
d) water at the bottom of a waterfall?
e) a stretched bow with the arrow about to be released?
f) the arrow half-way to the target?
g) a rock at the top of a cliff?
h) the rock falling, half-way down?

4 Use the internet, or an encyclopedia, to find out about the life of James Joule.

Running out of energy

Learn about:
● energy sources
● fossil fuels

We need energy for running our homes, transport and factories. Most of this energy comes from burning **fuels**.
Fuels store energy.

▶ Make a list of all the fuels you can think of. The picture will help you.

▶ Write down 3 things about your life that would be different if we did not have these fuels.

Coal, oil and natural gas are called **fossil fuels**. They were made from plants and animals that lived on Earth many millions of years ago.

▶ Look at the table of data and interpret it to answer these questions:

a Which fuel is easiest to set alight?

b Which fuel burns most cleanly?

c Which fossil fuel is solid?

d Which is the liquid that gives us petrol?

e Which fuel gives most energy when 1 gram of it is burned?

f The price of these fuels varies from year to year, but from the table which is the cheapest?

Fossil fuel	Easy to light?	Burns cleanly?	Amount of energy released	Approx. amount of energy for £1
natural gas	very easy	yes	55 kJ per gram	230 000 kJ
oil	yes	no	45 kJ per gram	250 000 kJ
coal	no	no	30 kJ per gram	300 000 kJ

Fossil fuels are **non-renewable** sources of energy. Once we have used them up, they are gone for ever!

▶ On the time-chart find:
● the year you were born
● where we are now
● the year when you will be 40 years old
● the year in which you will be 60.

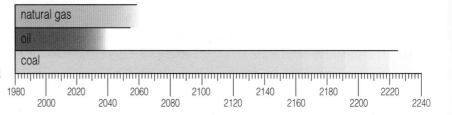

g From this chart, what do you notice about the fuels?

h What can you predict about your life when you are 60?

▶ There are other sources of energy called **renewable** sources. For example: energy from the wind (as in a windmill).

i How many other renewable sources of energy can you name? Make a list.

Energy consumption

Fossil fuels are used in some power stations to make electricity.

We can also get energy from:
- **nuclear power stations**. They use uranium but this is getting scarce.
- **hydro-electric power stations**. They use the potential energy from water stored in high dams.
- **biomass**. This is the energy stored in growing plants, such as wood.

▶ Look at the pie-charts and interpret them to answer these questions:

j List the energy sources used in the UK.

k What was the percentage for natural gas in the UK? Where do you use natural gas in school?

l Which were the biggest sources of energy for the UK in 2000?

m Which was the smallest source of energy for the UK? Why is this?

n Which source was not used in the UK?

o Which of the sources are *renewable*?

p In your group, compare the two charts and suggest some reasons why you think they are different.

q *Predict* what you think the world pie-chart will look like when you are 60.

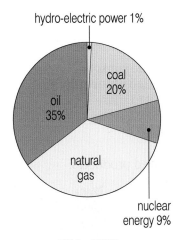

UK in 2000

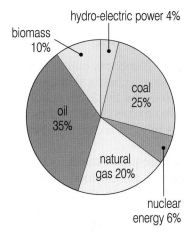

World in 2000

High tea

Imagine you are climbing a high mountain.
You will need to heat some snow, to make some soup or tea.

You can take with you either a **candle** or a **spirit-burner**, to heat the snow.
Plan an investigation to find out which is better.

- Sketch the equipment you would use.
- How will you make sure that your test is as fair as possible?
- How will you make your investigation safe to do?

---

1 Petrol, coal and potatoes are fuels. Explain how you could use each of these fuels to keep you warm.

2 Make a survey of all the fuels used in your home.

3 Make a leaflet for Year-6 children, explaining why it is important to conserve energy supplies, and how they can help.

4 Make a table showing how people could save fossil fuels. For example:

Action to be taken	How it saves fuel
Drive smaller cars	Uses less petrol

5 Make a list of the properties of an **ideal** fuel.

Things to do

Energy from the Sun

Learn about:
● energy in plants
● using solar energy

a Where does the Earth get most of its energy from**?**
b Think of all the things that happen because of the Sun. Make a list of as many as you can.

Making food

Green plants can capture the energy in the sunlight.
The green chemical in their leaves is called **chlorophyll**.
It *absorbs* the Sun's energy and uses it to make food.
It also makes oxygen for us to breathe.
This process is called **photo-synthesis**.

Because plants make food, they are called producers.
Animals eat this food – they are consumers.

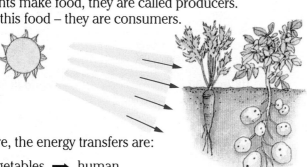

In this picture, the energy transfers are:

Sun ➡ vegetables ➡ human

This is called a **food-energy chain**.

Here are some food-energy chains that are in the wrong order. Write each one in the correct order.
c rabbit, Sun, grass, fox
d humans, grass, sheep, Sun
e thrush, Sun, cabbage, caterpillar

Biofuel

Plant and animal materials are called **biomass**.
As well as being food, biomass can give us energy in other ways:

● Wood is a fuel. It can be burnt to give energy for heating.

● In Brazil they grow sugar cane, and then use the sugar to make alcohol. The alcohol is then used in cars, instead of petrol.

● Rotting plants and animal manure can make a gas called methane.
This is like the gas you use in a Bunsen burner.
If the plants rot in a closed tank, called a **digester**, the gas can be piped away. This is often used in China and India:

▶ Design a digester to use straw and dung. Think about:
 ● It needs an air-tight tank.
 ● How will you get the gas out, to a cooker**?**
 ● How will you get the straw and dung in**?**
f Draw a sketch of your design and label it.

A cow-dung digester in India

Solar energy

The energy in the Sun's rays is called **solar energy**.

g Why is the Earth the only planet in the Solar System with life on it?

h Which parts of the Earth get the least energy?

▶ Look at these 3 ways of using solar energy, and answer the questions:

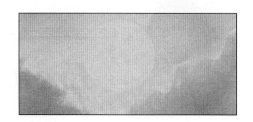

A **solar cell** transfers some of the sunlight into electricity.

In the photo, some solar cells are being used to run an electric water-pump:

You may have a calculator that uses a solar cell.

i What are the advantages and disadvantages of a solar-powered calculator?

j Why are solar cells not widely used?

A **solar cooker** has a curved mirror, to focus the Sun's rays:

k Is the mirror convex or concave?

▶ Design your own solar cooker. Think about:
- Should the mirror be large or small?
- Should the mirror be fixed or adjustable?
- Where should you put the pan or kettle?

l Draw a sketch of your design and label it.

Some houses have a **solar panel** on the roof. Water in the panel is heated by the Sun, and stored in a tank:

▶ Design your own solar panel system. Think about:
- Hot water rises, cold water falls.
- Black cars get hotter in the Sun than white cars.
- Objects get hotter behind glass (like in a greenhouse).

m Draw a sketch of your design and label it.

▶ Use black and silver trays to investigate the rise in temperature of different objects left in sunlight.

---

1 Copy and complete:
a) Energy from the Sun is called .... energy.
b) Green plants contain a chemical called .... This absorbs the Sun's .... and uses it to make .... and .... This process is called ....
c) The materials that plants and animals are made from, are called ....

2 How does a greenhouse use solar energy to help gardeners?

3 For each of these food-energy chains, write them in the correct order:
a) chicken, Sun, human, corn
b) seaweed, Sun, seagull, snail
c) ladybird, rose, greenfly, Sun
d) grasshopper, lizard, Sun, grass, hawk
e) bee, human, flower, Sun, honey
f) dead leaves, frog, Sun, earthworm, tree

4 What are:
a) the advantages, and
b) the disadvantages of a solar panel?

Things to do

From fossils to fuels

Learn about:
- how fuels were formed
- making electricity
- discussing nuclear energy

▶ What is a **fuel?**
Write down as many fuels as you can think of.

▶ Coal, oil and natural gas are important fuels. Read the sections below and then answer questions **a** to **j**.

A fossil in coal

How was coal formed?

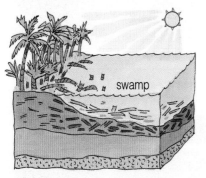

300 million years ago, plants store the Sun's energy. Dead plants fall into swampy water. The mud stops them from rotting away.

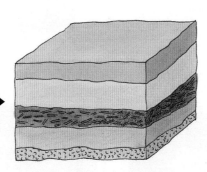

As the mud piles up, it squashes the plants.
After millions of years under pressure, the mud becomes rock and the plants become **coal**.

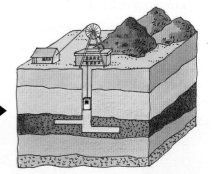

To reach the coal, miners dig shafts and tunnels. There is probably enough coal to last 300 years.
Fossils of plants are sometimes found in lumps of coal.

How was oil formed?

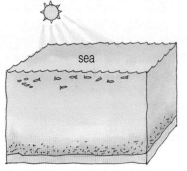

Tiny animals and plants live in the sea. When they die, they fall into the mud and sand at the bottom, and don't rot away.

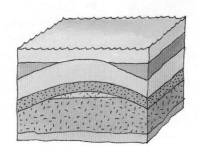

Over millions of years they get buried deeper by the mud and sand.
Pressure changes the mud and sand to rock, and the dead animals and plants become **crude oil** and **natural gas**.

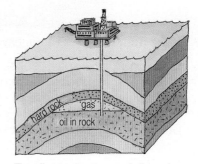

The oil can move upwards through some rocks, but if it meets a layer of hard rock it is trapped (with the gas).
An oil rig can drill down to release it.
There is enough oil to last about 40 years.

a What is a fossil?

b Why are coal, oil and gas called fossil fuels?

c Explain in your own words how coal was formed.

d Give 2 similarities and 2 differences between the way coal was formed and the way oil was formed.

e Diana says, "The energy stored in coal, oil and gas all comes from the Sun." Explain this statement.

f Oil, coal and gas are called **non-renewable** resources. What do you think this means?

g Why will fossil fuels eventually run out?

h How old will you be when the oil runs out?

i Why is coal usually found in layers?

j Why are some rocks called sedimentary rocks?

Renewable and non-renewable

Some sources of energy are **renewable**.
For example, wood. It can be burnt, but a new tree can be planted.
Solar energy is also a renewable resource.

However coal, oil and gas are **non-renewable** resources. Once we have used them up, they are gone forever.

Uranium is another non-renewable resource. It is used in nuclear power stations. Supplies of uranium will run out eventually.

Making electricity

The graphs show the sources of energy used to generate electricity in 3 countries:

k Which country generates the most electricity**?**

l List the energy sources used to make electricity in the UK.

m Hydroelectric sources are not used much in the UK. Why is this**?**

n Which is the main source in Norway**?** Why is this**?**

o What do you notice about the use of nuclear power in the 3 countries**?**

p Which of the sources is renewable**?**

q Coal has been used a lot in the UK, but coal-fired power stations can produce a lot of **acid rain**. What would be your solution to this problem, taking into account:
  i) the environment**?**
  ii) coal-miners and their families**?**

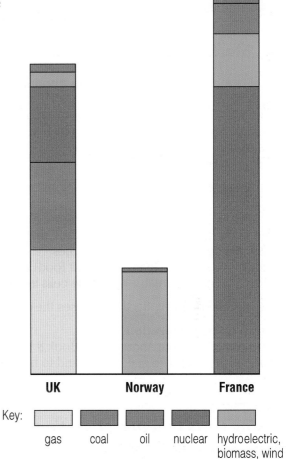

| | | |
| UK | Norway | France |

Key:

| gas | coal | oil | nuclear | hydroelectric, biomass, wind |

The nuclear debate

The world is running out of energy, but many people are against the use of nuclear energy.

In a group, use the Help Sheets to discuss your ideas *for* or *against* using nuclear energy.

Things to do

1 Copy and complete:
a) Coal, oil and . . . . are fossil . . . . They have taken . . . . of years to form.
b) Coal, oil, gas and uranium are non- . . . . sources of energy.
c) Some renewable sources of energy are:

2 Explain in your own words how oil and natural gas were formed.

3 Why is it important to avoid wastage of fossil fuels?

4 Make a table to show how people could save non-renewable fuels. For example:

Action to be taken	How it saves fuel
don't overfill the kettle	uses less electricity

Burning fuels

Learn about:
● energy in living things
● how power stations work
● comparing foods

▶ What fuels do you use in your home? Make a list.

▶ Look at this picture of a *match* burning:

Wood is a fuel. It has potential energy stored in it.
This energy can only be transferred if the fuel burns with
the oxygen in the air.
It is a chemical reaction.

Burning fuels are used in power stations and in car engines.

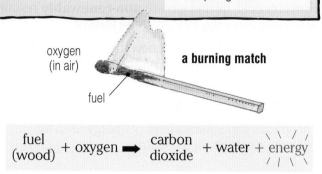

oxygen
(in air)

a burning match

fuel

fuel
(wood) + oxygen ➡ carbon
dioxide + water + energy

The *cells* in your body 'burn' the food that you eat
– but of course there aren't any flames!
Your blood carries sugar (from your food) and oxygen
(from the air you breathe) to all the cells in your body:

The *same* chemical reaction releases the energy.

This is called **respiration**.
(You will learn more about this in Book 8.)
You use the energy to keep warm and to move around.

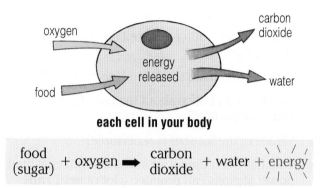

carbon
dioxide

oxygen

energy
released

water

food

each cell in your body

food
(sugar) + oxygen ➡ carbon
dioxide + water + energy

Using fuels in a power station

Follow the diagram to see how fuel is burned, to generate electricity:

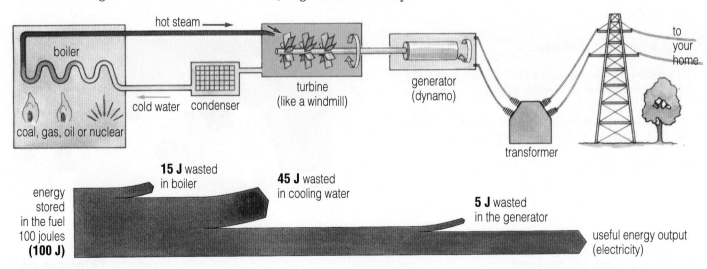

hot steam ➡

boiler

cold water   condenser

turbine
(like a windmill)

generator
(dynamo)

transformer

to
your
home

coal, gas, oil or nuclear

15 J wasted
in boiler

45 J wasted
in cooling water

5 J wasted
in the generator

energy
stored
in the fuel
100 joules
(100 J)

useful energy output
(electricity)

a What does the boiler do?

b What does the steam do to the turbine?

c What does the generator do?

d For every 100 joules of energy in the fuel, how much comes out as useful energy?

e Where is most energy wasted? Can you think of a way of using this wasted energy?

Comparing engines

A car engine burns fuel. The energy from the fuel makes the engine turn, so the car moves.

A human body is also a kind of engine:

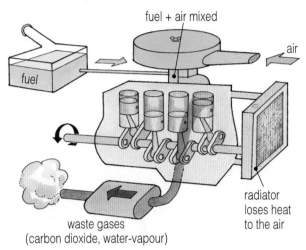

fuel + air mixed

air

fuel

waste gases
(carbon dioxide, water-vapour)

radiator
loses heat
to the air

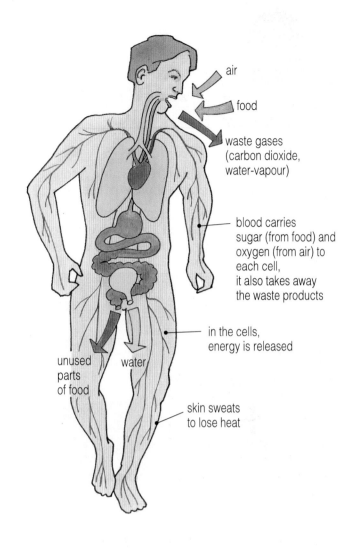

air

food

waste gases
(carbon dioxide,
water-vapour)

blood carries
sugar (from food) and
oxygen (from air) to
each cell,
it also takes away
the waste products

in the cells,
energy is released

unused
parts
of food

water

skin sweats
to lose heat

For each question **f** to **l**, write down the answer, first for the **car engine** and then for the **human engine**.

f What fuel does the engine use?

g What does it use the fuel for?

h Where is the fuel used ('burned') in the engine?

i How does the engine get its oxygen?

j How does the engine get rid of unwanted heat?

k What waste substances are produced in the engine?

l How does the engine get rid of these waste products?

Investigating sweeteners

Plan an investigation to compare the **amount of energy** in some **sugar** and in some **artificial sweetener**.

- How will you make them burn?
- What will you do with the energy from the burning fuel?
- How will you make it a fair test? And safe!

Ask your teacher to check your plan, and then do the investigation.

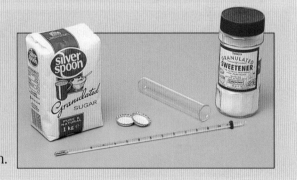

Things to do

1 Copy and complete:
a) In order to burn, a fuel needs . . . .
It usually gets this from the . . . .
b) The word equation for a fuel burning is:
c) In the cells in my body, energy is released when sugar (from my . . . .) reacts with . . . . (from the . . . . I breathe).
d) This is called . . . .
e) The word equation for this is:

2 Do a flow-chart to show how the energy in a coal-mine makes a cup of tea for you.

3 Draw an Energy Diagram for:
a) a burning match,
b) a cell in your body.

4 Explain the correct way to deal with:
a) a chip-pan fire,   b) a petrol fire,
c) an electric blanket on fire.

Energy for ever?

Learn about:
- renewable energy sources
- solving problems creatively

▶ What is meant by a **non-renewable** resource?
Name 4 non-renewable sources of energy.

What is a **renewable** source of energy?
You have already studied 2 renewable sources,
biofuel and *solar energy* (on pages 126–127).
Here are some more:

Wind energy
Windmills have been used for centuries.
Modern wind-turbines are huge. One advantage is that the wind blows most when we need more energy – in winter.

Why does this energy come originally from the Sun?

Geothermal energy
This geyser is spurting out hot water. This is because deep inside the Earth it is very hot.
If a very deep hole is drilled, cold water can be piped down, to return as hot water or steam.

Wave energy
Waves are caused by the wind. They contain a lot of energy but it is hard to make use of it. Scientists have tried many ways to make electricity from it. One idea is to have floats that move up and down with the waves and so turn a generator.

Why does this energy come originally from the Sun?

Hydro-electric energy
Water stored by a dam has potential energy.
When it runs down-hill, its kinetic energy can turn a turbine or a water-wheel. This can turn a generator to make electricity.

Why does the energy come originally from the Sun?
Why is this resource impossible in some countries?

Tidal energy
The tides are caused by the pull of the Moon and Sun.
In some places there are very high tides.
The water can be trapped behind a barrier, like a dam:
Then it can be used like hydro-electric energy.

Joule Island

Joule Island is a remote island, in the Pacific Ocean.
You are in a team of 30 scientists who will be staying on the island for 3 years to study it.
Your task is to provide all the energy that the team will need.

Study the island:

a There are no fossil fuels on the island, and it is 500 km to the mainland. What would be the advantages and disadvantages of setting up a power station which used coal or oil?

b What renewable energy resources are there on the island?

c Which natural resource on the island should be carefully conserved?

The island has sunny days but cold nights.
The wind blows most days, but not in summer.
The hot springs are at a temperature of 80°C.

d The team is going to build huts to live in. Name 2 ways in which the huts could be heated.

e Design a way of supplying hot water for washing.

f Design a way of supplying energy for cooking food.

g The team has a refrigerator for medicines which have to be kept cool at all times, day and night. Design a way of supplying electricity continuously for the refrigerator.

h Your teacher will give you a picture of the island. Mark on the picture:
  • where you would build the huts, and
  • where you would build any energy installations you have designed, and
  • show how the energy would be transferred to the huts.

i When summer comes, you find that the fresh-water sources tend to dry up. How does this affect your energy plan? Design a way to get over this.

j For some experiments on the island you need some gas for a Bunsen burner. Describe 2 ways to provide this.

Things to do

1 Copy and complete:
a) Fossil fuels like coal, ... , and natural gas will eventually run out. They are non-. . . . resources.
b) Nuclear energy is also a . . . . resource.
c) Other energy resources are called . . . .
d) The 7 renewable forms of energy are:

2 Which of the 7 renewable sources get their energy originally from the Sun?

3 Find out how scientists have tried to make use of wave power. Explain one of their inventions.

4 Design the scientists' huts for Joule Island. You should design them so that:
• they have sleeping, leisure and work areas, and
• they will be cool during the day and warm at night.

Questions

1 Draw Energy Diagrams for:
a) a torch
b) a bonfire burning
c) a boy kicking a football.

2 A car engine is only 25% efficient. Of every 100 joules in the petrol, only 25 J actually make the car move.
a) What happens to the other 75 joules?
b) Draw an Energy Diagram for the car.

3 Draw a food-energy chain to show how the energy in a cheeseburger comes from the Sun to:
a) the cheese
b) the bread.

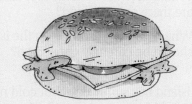

4 In a solar cell, for every 100 joules of solar energy shining on it, only 10 J is transferred to useful energy in electricity.
a) What happens to the other 90 joules?
b) Draw an Energy Diagram of this, with the width of the arrows to scale. Label it.

5 a) Think about what life would be like without coal, oil, or natural gas. (Remember that petrol and plastics come from oil.) You can present your ideas in a list, or in a story, or on a poster.
b) Make a list of the ways that your school could reduce its energy bills.

6 When you switch on a light, it is the result of a long chain of events. These are listed below, in the wrong order. Write them down in the correct order.
A   plants take in energy from the Sun
B   coal is burnt in oxygen (in air)
C   water is heated, to make steam
D   the Sun produces energy
E   plants change to coal over millions of years
F   steam makes a turbine turn
G   the generator produces electricity
H   electricity heats up the lamp and it shines
I   the turbine turns a generator
J   electricity travels through wires to your home

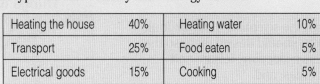

7 A typical British family uses energy like this:

Heating the house	40%	Heating water	10%
Transport	25%	Food eaten	5%
Electrical goods	15%	Cooking	5%

a) Draw a pie-chart or a bar-chart to show this information.
b) Where should they look first in order to save money?

Electrical circuits

7J

Electricity is important to all of us.
Our lives would be very different without it.

We use electricity to transfer energy from one place to another.
We use it for heating and for lighting.

We can transfer energy by series and parallel circuits, taking care to work safely.

Switch on!

Electricity is a very useful way of getting energy. Sometimes we use a **battery** and sometimes we use **mains** electricity. Mains electricity can be dangerous – you must not use it in these experiments.

▶ Make a list of things in your home that use electricity from a battery or from the mains.

▶ Look at the **circuit** shown here.

Below it is a **circuit diagram**, which shows the same circuit, in symbols.

Find the symbol for: a) the **battery** (or '**cell**')
　　　　　　　　　　 b) the **lamp bulb**
　　　　　　　　　　 c) the **switch**.

▶ Copy this circuit diagram and label the symbols.

▶ Now use the equipment to make the circuit.

What do you have to do to make the bulb light up**?**

We say there is an electric **current** flowing in the circuit. A current can flow *only if there is a complete circuit* with no gaps in it.

▶ Look carefully at a switch. What happens when you press it? How does it work**?**

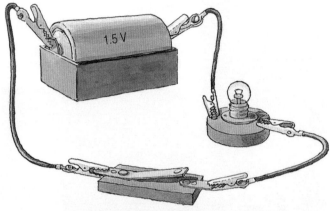

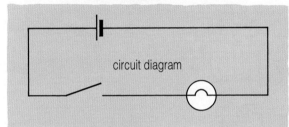
circuit diagram

Looking at cells

The photo shows the inside of a **cell**:

The cell can provide energy in order to light a bulb.
The cell's energy comes from the chemicals that the cell is made of.
When the chemicals have been used up (reacted), it stops working.

A cell has a positive (+) terminal and a negative (−) terminal.

If 2 or more cells are connected together, they are called a **battery**. The cells are connected with the + of one cell connected to the − of the next, as shown:

If two 1.5 volt cells are connected like this, the total voltage is 3 volts. This will make more current flow. It will light a bulb more brightly, because it transfers more energy to the bulb.

A cell transfers chemical energy to electrical energy

a 1.5 volt cell

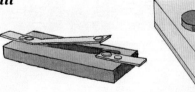
a battery of 2 cells

Electric games

Choose *one* of these games and draw a detailed diagram of how you would make it.
Show your plan to your teacher, and then make your game.

Steady hand game

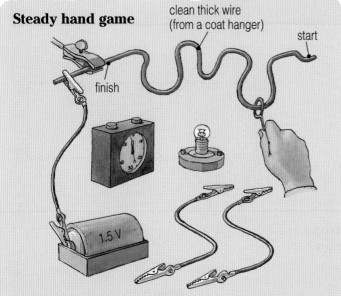

Is your hand steady enough for you to be a surgeon or a vet?

- How many seconds does it take you?
- Can you do it with your other hand?
- Can you count backwards from 99 at the same time?

Quiz game

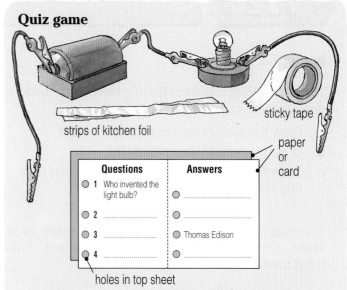

- How can you use the kitchen foil to connect a 'Question' hole to the correct 'Answer' hole (but so it can't be seen)?
- What can you use to insulate the strips of foil from each other?
- Make up your own science questions (and answers) to test your friends.

▶ Write down how your game works, using these words:

battery	**connecting wire**	**complete circuit**	**electric current**	**conductor**	**insulator**

1 Copy and complete:
a) Mains electricity can be very . . . .
b) When a bulb lights up it shows that an electric . . . . is flowing.
c) For an electric current to flow, there must be a . . . . circuit, with no gaps in it.

2 Answering carefully,
a) Draw and label the circuit symbols for
   i) a battery   ii) a bulb   iii) a switch.
b) Explain what happens when you operate a switch.
c) Explain how 2 cells can light a bulb more brightly than one cell.

3 Suppose you wake up tomorrow morning and find there is no electricity at all in the world. How would your life be different?

4 Mr. Smith is deaf and can't hear his door-bell.
a) Draw a circuit diagram to show how you would connect a bulb to light up when a visitor presses the switch.
b) How would you change it to light another bulb in his kitchen as well as one in his living-room? Draw a circuit diagram.

5 Design a poster to warn young children not to poke at mains sockets or electric fires.

6 Jack set up the circuit shown on page 136, but it does not work. Write a list of checks he could make to find the fault.

7 Find out what you can about the life of Michael Faraday.

Things to do

Series and parallel

Learn about:
● using a 'model' to explain
● series and parallel circuits

▶ Look at this diagram:

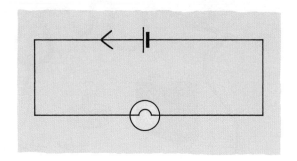

There is an electric current flowing through the battery and through the wires in the bulb.

a Draw the symbol for a battery, and label it.

b Draw the symbol for a bulb (a lamp).

c Draw this circuit diagram, and mark arrows on it everywhere you think there is a current.

Scientists have discovered that electricity is made up of **electrons**. These are tiny particles, even smaller than atoms. The electrons travel through the wires.

Let's look at a 'model' to help us explain electrical circuits. An electric current is rather like water flowing through a pipe. Look at this diagram of the central-heating pipes in a house:

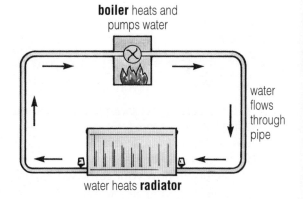

boiler heats and pumps water

water flows through pipe

water heats **radiator**

d Which part of the diagram do you think is like a **battery**? (Hint: a battery pushes electrons round a circuit.)

e Which part of the diagram do you think is most like a **bulb**? (Hint: a bulb is heated up by the electrons going through it.)

This model is not perfect. We say it has limitations.

f Think of a limitation of this pumped-water model. (Hint: what happens if you cut a wire or cut a pipe?)

Series circuit

The water goes through the boiler, and then the same water goes through the radiator.
We say they are **in series**.

In the same way, the electrons go through the battery and then they go through the bulb, and then back to the battery.
It is a **series circuit**.

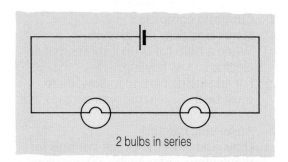

2 bulbs in series

▶ Connect up this series circuit:

g Do both bulbs light up? Is a current going through both bulbs?

h Now unscrew **one** of the bulbs. What happens? Why does this happen?

i Christmas tree lights are often connected in series. What happens then if **one** of the bulbs breaks?

j How do you know that the lights in your house are not wired in series?

Parallel circuits

Look at this circuit, and its circuit diagram below:

This is a **parallel circuit**.
There are two paths for the current to flow along, with a bulb in each path.
We say the two paths are **in parallel**.

When the electrons travel from the battery, *some* of them go through bulb **A** and *the rest* of them go through bulb **B**.

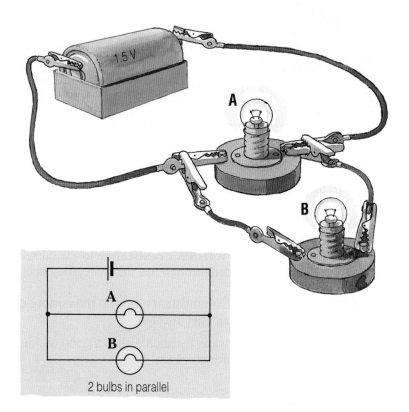

▶ Connect up this parallel circuit:

k Do both bulbs light up? Is a current going round both paths?

l Now unscrew *one* of the bulbs. Why does the other bulb stay on?

m Are the lights in your house connected in series or in parallel? How do you know?

n Design a circuit to supply current to 5 bulbs, one for each of the 5 rooms in a house.

2 bulbs in parallel

Analysing circuits

Here is a circuit diagram for 2 lights in a doll's house:

Use your finger to follow the path of the electrons from the battery through the bulb **P** and back to the battery. *If your finger has to go through a switch, then this switch is needed to put on the light.*

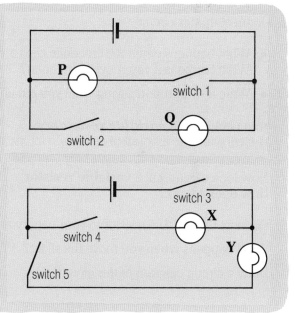

o Which switch is needed to switch on bulb **P**?

p Which switch is needed for bulb **Q**?

Use the same method to find out the answers to these questions:

q How would you switch on bulb **X**?

r How would you switch on bulb **Y**?

s Are the bulbs **X** and **Y** connected in series or in parallel?

---

1 Copy and complete:
a) In an electric circuit, tiny . . . . move through the wires.
b) If the same current goes through two bulbs, then the bulbs are in . . . .
c) If the current splits up to go through two different paths, we say the paths are in . . . .

2 Design a burglar alarm so that if a burglar steps on your door-mat, an electric bell rings.

3 A torch contains a battery, a switch and a bulb in series.
a) Draw a circuit diagram of this.
Suppose your torch is broken.
b) Describe, with a diagram, how you could test the bulb.
c) How could you test the battery?

4 Jim needs a circuit for his caravan, so that 3 bulbs, each with its own switch, can work from a car battery. Draw a circuit diagram for Jim.

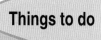

Things to do

Getting hot

Learn about:
● using an ammeter
● resistance and fuses

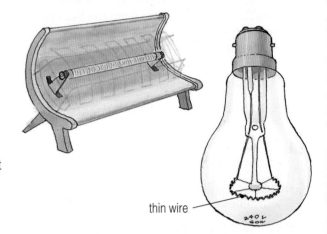

thin wire

We often use electricity to heat things.

▶ Make a list of all the things in your house that use electricity to get hot.

The thin wire inside a light bulb glows white-hot.
This is because the thin wire has a **resistance** to the current.
As the electrons are forced through this thin wire, they heat it up.

An insulator has a very high resistance, and so the current cannot flow. The electrons cannot get through.

A copper wire has a very low resistance. It is a good conductor.
The electrons can get through easily.

Investigating resistance

Connect up this circuit:

● What happens when the crocodile clips are close together? What happens if you move them apart?

● Write a short report saying what you did and what you found.

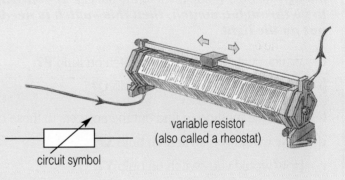

nichrome wire

Your circuit has a *variable resistance*.
You can vary the amount of resistance it has.

Now look carefully at a **variable resistor**:
How does it work?

Connect the variable resistor to your battery and bulb.

What happens when you move the slider? Why?

Draw a circuit diagram of this circuit.

circuit symbol

variable resistor
(also called a rheostat)

Now look at an **ammeter**.
An ammeter measures the size of a current. It measures it in **amperes** (also called **amps** or **A**).

Connect your battery, bulb, variable resistor and an ammeter in series. *Take care* to connect the red (+) terminal on the ammeter to the + (the button) on the battery.

What happens as you vary the resistance?

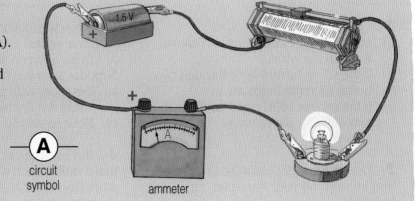

Ⓐ circuit symbol

ammeter

Fuses for safety

▶ Connect up this circuit:

Put on safety spectacles. Then look carefully at the thin wire while you press the switch. What happens?

▶ Write down what you think is happening, using the words:

> **battery**   **complete circuit**
> **current**   **amperes**   **heating**

very
thin
wire

The thin wire has melted or **fused**.
When it fuses, it stops the current flowing.
It is a safety device. We call it a **fuse**.

A fuse is a weak part of the circuit. It breaks if there is a fault which lets too much current flow.

Every mains plug has a fuse inside it.
You can buy fuses with different ratings, such as 3 amp or 13 amp.
A table lamp or TV needs a 3 A fuse.
An electric fire needs a 13 A fuse.

thin wire

3A

13A

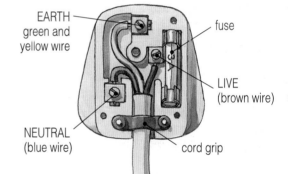

Using the wrong fuse in a TV?

Mains plug

▶ Look carefully at the diagram of a mains plug:
It is very **very** important that the coloured wires are connected to the correct places.

Why is the cord grip important?

▶ Draw a safety poster to help you remember the correct way to wire a plug.

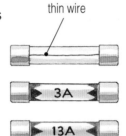

EARTH
green and
yellow wire

fuse

LIVE
(brown wire)

NEUTRAL
(blue wire)

cord grip

---

1 Copy and complete:
a) A good conductor has a . . . . resistance.
   An insulator has a . . . . resistance.
b) The current in a circuit can be varied using a . . . . resistor (also called a . . . .).
c) An ammeter measures the . . . . in a circuit, in . . . . or A.
d) A fuse . . . . if the current is too big.
e) In a mains plug the brown wire is called the . . . . wire and must go to the fuse.
   The green/yellow wire is the . . . . wire and must go to the . . . . pin.
   The blue wire is the . . . . wire.

2 Where might you use a variable resistor (rheostat) in a theatre? Draw a circuit diagram suitable for a toy theatre.

3 Draw a circuit diagram of the ammeter circuit that you used. Label the symbols.

4 What can you say about the thickness of the wire in a 3 A fuse compared with a 13 A fuse?
Which one has the bigger resistance?

5 What might happen if you put a 13 A fuse in a plug for a TV, and the TV was faulty?

6 Draw a circuit with a battery, 2 bulbs in parallel, each controlled by a switch, and an ammeter measuring the total current taken by the bulbs.
Where would you put a variable resistor to dim one of the bulbs?

Things to do

Current affairs

▶ Look at this circuit diagram:

a What does each symbol stand for?

b What happens if the circuit is not complete?

We say that the ammeter and the bulb are **in series**.
Tiny **electrons** are moving through the wires.

c Draw a circuit diagram for a battery (cell) and 2 bulbs in series.

d What can you say about the brightness of the 2 bulbs?
What can you say about the current through the 2 bulbs?
What happens if one of the bulbs breaks?

e What is an **insulator**?

f Draw a diagram of a circuit you could use to test if an object is an insulator or a conductor.

g Now draw a circuit diagram for a battery and 2 bulbs **in parallel**.

h What happens if one of the bulbs breaks?

A circuit contains a battery, a switch, and 3 bulbs labelled X, Y, and Z. Bulbs X and Y are in series, and bulb Z is in parallel with X. The switch controls only bulb Z.

i Draw a circuit diagram of this.

j When all the bulbs are lit, which one is the brightest?

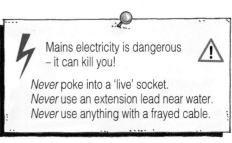

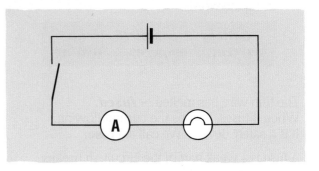

Mains electricity is dangerous
– it can kill you!

Never poke into a 'live' socket.
Never use an extension lead near water.
Never use anything with a frayed cable.

Research

Find out and prepare a brief account on one of the following topics:

- The work of Galvani and Volta in developing our ideas about electricity.

- The use of defibrillators and pacemakers in hospitals.

Currents in a circuit

Connect up this circuit:

Take care to connect the ammeter the correct way round (+ of ammeter to + of battery).

Measure the current in the circuit.
Now move your ammeter to measure the current in different parts of the circuit.

k Are the components in series or in parallel?

l What can you say about the current in different parts of the circuit?

Now set up the bulbs in parallel.

m Predict the current at different points in the parallel circuit.

Now measure the currents to test your predictions.

n What did you find out about the currents in parallel circuits?

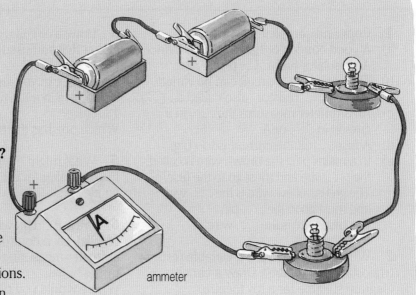

ammeter

Making a fire-alarm

A **bi-metallic strip** is made of 2 metals fastened together.
When it is heated, the metals get longer. They *expand*.

But one metal expands more than the other.
What happens to the strip? Try it. Explain what you see.

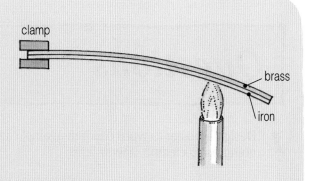

Design a fire-alarm using a bi-metallic strip.

- Think about how you can use it to ring a bell or light a warning lamp.
- Draw a circuit diagram of your design.

Ask your teacher to check your circuit. Then build it and test it.

Sketch a drawing of your fire-alarm. Describe how it works.
How could your design be improved?

You have used the bi-metallic strip as a **sensor**.

o How could the strip be changed to make it more sensitive?

Inventing

p Draw your fire-alarm circuit with a test button (switch) so that the bell can be tested regularly.

q How could you change your fire-alarm design to warn you if something got too cold? Can you think of a use for this?

r Design a circuit that will put on a heater if the room is too cold, and put on a fan if the room is too hot.
Can you do this using just one battery in the circuit?

s Where the hot-water pipe enters a central-heating radiator, there is often a valve so you can turn off the radiator.
Design a valve that turns off the radiator when it gets hot, . . . and turns it back on again when it cools.

Professor Messer invents a candle gadget
that gives him time to get into bed!
How does it work?

---

1 Copy and complete:
a) If the same current goes through two bulbs, then the bulbs are in . . . .
b) If the current splits up to go through two different paths, then we say the paths are in . . . .
c) A good conductor has a . . . . resistance. An insulator has a . . . . resistance.
d) An ammeter measures the . . . . in a circuit, in . . . . or A.
e) A bi-metallic strip is made of two . . . . When it is heated, the metal that . . . . more is on the outside of the curve.

2 Draw circuit diagrams of these:
a) A battery (cell) and a switch connected to 2 bulbs, a variable resistor and an ammeter all in series.
b) Two batteries (cells) in series, connected to 2 bulbs wired in parallel, an ammeter to measure the total current taken by the bulbs, and a switch to control each bulb.

3 Draw a circuit diagram to show how 3 lamps can be switched on and off separately but dimmed all together.

Things to do

Questions

1 Design a poster to warn children against climbing electric pylons or going on to electric railway lines.

2 Describe a 'model' that helps us to understand what happens in electrical circuits. Using your model, try to explain the difference between *current* and *energy transfer* in circuits.

3 Draw a labelled diagram of a light bulb.
Which parts are: a) insulators? b) conductors?

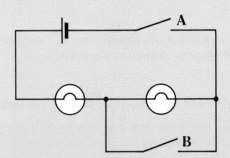

4 In the circuit shown in the diagram, what happens if:
a) switch **A** only is closed?
b) switch **B** only is closed?
c) **A** and **B** are closed?
d) Are the bulbs in series or in parallel?

5 a) An electric saw needs 2 switches for safety.
Design a circuit so that both switches must be 'on' to start the saw, but only one switch need be turned 'off' to stop the saw.
b) A bank needs an alarm system.
Design a circuit that has a battery and an alarm bell that can be switched on by 2 separate push-buttons
c) Which of these two circuits (a or b) could you use for door-bell switches at your front door and back door?

6 This diagram shows one kind of ammeter. What are the readings **a**, **b**, **c**, **d**?

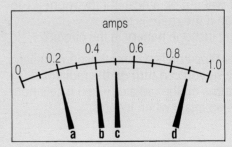

7 Draw a circuit diagram to show how two 6 volt bulbs can be lit brightly from two 3 volt batteries.

8 Each of the pictures below shows an unsafe situation.
For each one:
i) write a sentence about what is wrong, and
ii) say what should be done to make it safe.

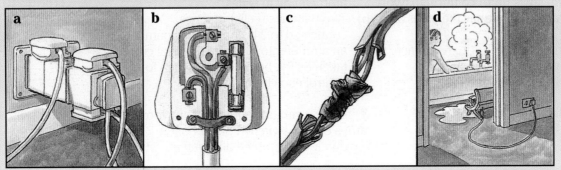

Forces and their effects

Your life is full of forces.

Everything that you do needs a force.
To lift your pen needs a force.
To turn the page needs a force

In the photo, the people are being pulled down the slide by the force of gravity. And they are being slowed by another force – the force of friction.

In this unit you can investigate forces, to find out what they can do and how to measure them.

In this unit:

Using forces

Learn about:
● forces, including weight
● measuring a force

   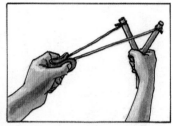

All these people are using **forces**.

▶ Look at the pictures above and find the force in each one.

a Write down a list of words that describe the forces in the pictures. Your first word can be ***push***.

b Write down 5 things that you have done today using a force. Which muscles did you use**?**

Force-meters

▶ Look at diagrams 1 to 4, of some **force-meters**: They are sometimes called newton-meters or spring-balances.

Each one is measuring the size of a force. We measure the size of a force in **newtons** (also written as **N**).

c For each force-meter, write down the largest force that it can measure on its scale.

d What force is each one showing on its scale here**?**

e The apple is pulling down with a force called its **weight**. What is the weight of the apple**?**

The weight of this book is about 5 newtons.

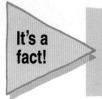

It's a fact!

An ant can pull with a force of $\frac{1}{1000}$ newton, a family car can push with 5000 newtons, and a moon-rocket exerts 30 million N.

Measuring forces

This table lists some jobs that need a force:

Copy out the table.

In each case, first make a **prediction** of how big you think the force will be. Write it down.

Then **measure** that force with a force-meter.
Take care to choose the right force-meter for each job.

	Size of force in newtons	
	Prediction	Actual
Lift a bag	20 ?	
Pull a stool along the floor		
Pull the stool more quickly		
Weigh a Bunsen burner		
Stretch a rubber-band to twice its length		
Open a door		

Finger strength

Plan an investigation to find the strength of people's finger muscles.

You can use bathroom scales as shown, and test several different people.

- How will you make sure it is a fair test?
- How will you record your results?
- How can you make your results more reliable?

Ask your teacher to check your plan, and then do your investigation.

Is there any pattern in your results?

Things to do

1 Copy and complete:
Forces can do 3 things. They can:
a) change the **size** or **shape** of an object (for example: squeezing a sponge)
b) change the speed of an object to make it move **faster** (for example: kicking a ball) or to make it move . . . . (for example: catching a ball)
c) change the **direction** of a moving object (e.g. a ball bouncing off a . . . .).

2 Sketch 3 of the pictures at the top of the opposite page and mark with an arrow where you think a force is acting.
For example:

3 Suppose you are given a ruler, a rubber-band, a paper-clip, some cotton thread and some sellotape. How could you use these to make your own force-meter?
Draw a diagram of your design and label it.

4 The newton is named after Sir Isaac Newton, a famous scientist who lived 300 years ago.

Do some research, and then write 3 paragraphs about him.

Floating and sinking

7K2

Learn about:
- upthrust in liquids
- balanced forces
- density

You know that some things *float* on water and some things *sink*.

The diagram shows some 'floaters' and some 'sinkers'.

▶ Draw up a table with 2 columns labelled 'floaters' and 'sinkers'. Fill in your table from the diagram.

▶ Which column do you think each of these would go in:
- stone?
- paper?
- soap?

Floating in the salty water of the Dead Sea in Israel

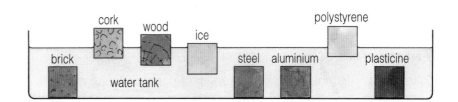

Why do things float or sink?

Hang a 'sinker' from a force-meter (spring-balance).

Write down the reading on the force-meter. This is the **weight** of the object. It is the pull of gravity by the Earth.

Push up your finger under the object. What happens to the force-meter reading?

Now gently lower the object into a beaker of water. What happens to the reading on the force-meter?

Copy the table and fill in the first line.

Repeat the experiment with a 'floater'. What do you find?

Try some more 'floaters' and 'sinkers'.

Can you see a rule which is true for all the things that float?

Name of object	Does it float or sink?	Weight in air (newtons)	Weight in water (newtons)	∴ Change in weight (newtons)
1.				
2.				

When an object is lowered into the water, the water pushes up on it. This force is called an **upthrust**.

If the object floats, the upthrust is **equal** to the weight. The two forces balance out.

They are **balanced forces**, and so the block of wood stays stationary in the water.

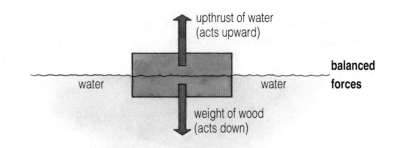

Density

A boat floats on water because of the upthrust.

If the boat weighs 10 000 newtons then the water must give an upthrust of 10 000 newtons.

A boat will float higher or lower depending on the **density** of the water.

Salty sea-water is **_more dense_** than fresh-water, so a boat floats higher in the salty sea than in a fresh-water lake.

To calculate the density of something you can use this formula:

$$\text{density} = \frac{\text{mass}}{\text{volume}}$$

The volume of 100 g of water is 100 cm^3. What is the density of water**?**

If an object has a density of more than 1 g/cm^3 (the density of water) then it will sink in water.

A helium balloon can float in air because the air gives it a small upthrust

Investigating boats

Design and build a boat that will support as much weight as possible.

You can use:
either   50 grams of plasticine (this weighs half a newton = 0.5 N)
_or_   a piece of kitchen foil of size 10 cm × 10 cm.

Your boat should: • float
                    • be stable (not fall over)
                    • carry a cargo.

For cargo you can use coins, paper-clips, marbles or small weights.

Try out different designs. Sketch them to keep a record.

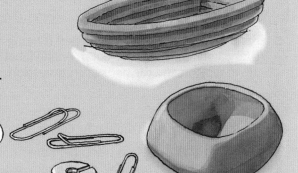

A challenge! Whose boat can carry the heaviest cargo**?**

---

1 Copy and complete:
a) Weight is a . . . . caused by the pull of . . . .
b) An object placed in water has a force called . . . . pushing up on it.
c) When an object floats, the upthrust is . . . . to the weight of the object. The two forces are . . . .

2 A steel block sinks in water. A steel ship floats. Try to explain why they are different.

3 Who was Archimedes? What did he do?

4 Ships have marks on their sides called **Plimsoll lines**. They show the levels at which the ship should float in different waters.

Look at this diagram.

Which mark (A or B) do you think is for:
a) fresh-water in a lake?
b) sea-water?

Things to do

Bending, stretching

Learn about:
- making predictions
- stretching springs
- interpreting graphs

▶ Choose one of these 2 investigations, and do it.
If you have time, you can do the other one.

Bending beams

▶ Bridges need to be safe and strong.
Look at this photo of a beam bridge:

a Write down 3 materials that a beam bridge could be made from.

b Name 3 materials that you would not use to build a bridge.

A bridge is a structure. In the structure some parts are being squashed.
This is called **compression**. The tiny particles are pushed closer together.

➡COMPRESSION⬅

Other parts of the bridge are being stretched apart.
They are in **tension**.

◀━TENSION▬➤

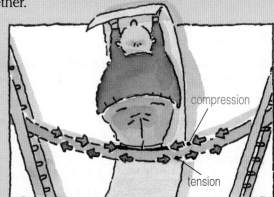

compression

tension

c What do you think is happening to the tiny particles
where the beam is in tension?

d Bend your ruler gently. Which part is being stretched?
Draw a diagram of your bent ruler and label the parts that
are in tension and the parts in compression.

Tara and her family are painting the ceiling:

Tara sees that the plank sags when her father stands on it.
It sags by a different amount when her baby sister stands on it.

- Write down what you think the sag of the plank depends on.
Give as much detail as you can. (This is your prediction.)
Try to include these words:

  | *weight* | *tension* | *compression* | *balanced forces* |

- Plan an investigation to see if your prediction is true.
(You could use a ruler as the plank.)
How will you record your results? ⚠

- Show your plan to your teacher, and then do it.

- When you have finished, write your report.
Make sure you try to explain your results.

Stretching springs

Springs are useful in many ways:

- Make a list of all the uses of springs that you can think of.

You can make your own spring by winding copper wire round a pencil:

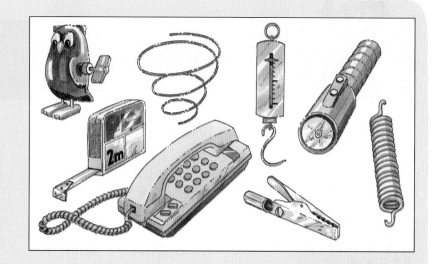

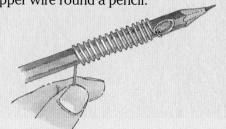

- Make a spring and then test it. Investigate how the length of your spring depends on the weight you hang on it.

- Plan your investigation carefully.
  How will you ensure your results are reliable?
  How will you record your results?

- Check your plan with your teacher, and then do it. Start with small weights and carry on until your spring loses its shape.

- Plot a graph of the length (or, better, the stretch 'extension') of your spring against the weight hanging on it.
  What do you notice?

- If you have time, repeat your investigation with
  – a spring made from iron wire or nichrome wire, or
  – a piece of elastic or a rubber band.
  What differences do you find on your line-graphs?

- Write a report of what you did and what you found out.

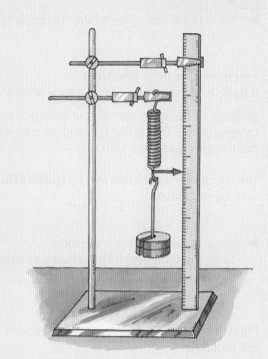

---

1 Peter likes to go fishing. He tested 2 new fishing lines by hanging weights on them. Here are his results:

weight (N)	0	5	10	15	20
length of line A (cm)	50	51	52	53	54
length of line B (cm)	50	52	54	56	58

a) What happens to the lines as he hangs weights on them?
b) How long is line A when the load weight is 20 N?
c) What is the load when line B is 52 cm?
d) Which of the lines was the more stretchy?
e) Both lines are made of nylon. Which do you think will be the stronger one?

2 Amy has long blonde hair and Ben has short black hair. Design an investigation to compare their hair strength.

3 Design a pram with springs so that it can travel over rough ground without shaking the baby.

4 Robert Hooke investigated springs over 300 years ago and wrote down Hooke's Law. Find out what is meant by Hooke's Law.

5 Use data shown in Question 1 to find the stretch ('extension') in each case. Plot 2 graphs (on the same axes). What do they show you?

Things to do

Friction and weight

Learn about:
- friction forces
- weight and mass
- newtons and kilograms

A small push can slide this book along the table. But why does it stop moving**?**

The book is touching the table, and they are both rough. When they rub together, the force of **friction** slows down the book.

Friction can be useful.
You can't walk unless there is friction between your shoes and the ground.

▶ List 3 other examples where friction is helpful to us.

Friction can be a problem.
If there is too much friction in a bicycle, then it is hard to pedal.

Because of friction some of your energy is used to warm up the moving parts. This is like rubbing your hands together to make them warm (see page 120).

You can make the friction less by **lubricating** the moving parts with oil or grease.

▶ Look at this photo of a bicycle:
Copy the table and fill in as many examples in each column as you can.

Friction is a **contact** force. It only happens if things are touching.

Other forces can act at a distance. For example: gravity.

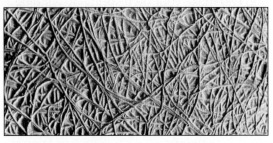

The surface of paper is rough (magnified ×100)

Riding a bicycle	
Friction is needed	Friction is not wanted
tyres on the road	

Weight

Weight is a force. It is the pull of **gravity**.

The Earth pulls down on the apple shown here, and on you.

The weight of an apple is about 1 newton (1 N).

Your weight is about 500 newtons (500 N).

Mass

In everyday life people talk about their 'weight' in **kilograms** (kg). This is wrong.

Kilograms are used to measure the **mass** of something.

Mass is the amount of matter in an object. It is not a force (but weight is).

Your mass will be the same on Earth or on the Moon, but your weight would change. Why**?**

Newtons and kilograms

Find the weight (in newtons) of different masses (in kilograms) using a force-meter.

Put your results in a table, and then draw a line-graph.

What is the relationship between kilograms and newtons?

What is the weight of 1 kg here on Earth?
Would it weigh more or less on the Moon?

Investigating friction

Imagine you are a shoe designer.
You have been asked to design some shoes that have a good 'grip' so that they won't slide easily.

Here are some things that make a shoe slide easily or not:

a the type of sole
b the ground surface or lubricant it is on
c the weight of the person in the shoe.

Choose **one** of these (**a**, **b** or **c**).

Then find out how changing it makes the shoe more or less easy to slide.

- What do you need to change and what do you need to measure?

- How will you ensure it is a fair test? What things (variables) do you need to keep the same each time?

- How will you make your results as reliable as possible?

- How will you record your results?

- What type of graph will you use?

What pattern do you find?
Present your findings to another group.

Air resistance (or **drag**) can be a problem.
Cars are **streamlined** to reduce air friction.

▶ How does the shape of dolphins help them?

---

1 Copy and complete:
a) Friction is a . . . . which tries to slow down objects when they rub together.
b) Friction can be reduced by . . . . the moving parts with oil. Air resistance can be reduced by . . . . the shape of a car.
c) Weight is a . . . . It is the pull of . . . . by the Earth.
d) Weight is measured in . . . . , while mass is measured in . . . .

2 Suppose you wake up tomorrow morning and find that there is no friction at all in your home.
Write a story to describe what could happen to you.

3 How can you reduce the friction in a bicycle?

4 Why is friction important for road safety? What can happen if the weather is
a) wet?   b) icy?

5 Make a table as shown:

Friction is needed	Friction is not wanted
catching a ball	swimming

Think about different sports, and list 5 examples in each column.

Things to do

Move it!

a push force
is needed to
start moving

To move something you have to apply a *force*.
You looked at this in lesson 7K1 (see page 147).

▶ Look at the cartoon:

a Which one needs the bigger force to start moving –
the heavy man or the little girl?

Now suppose both sledges are moving across the ice, at
the same speed.

b Which one needs a bigger force to stop it?

Objects usually slow down and stop, because of friction (see page 152).

c What happens to the sledge if there is very little friction?

d What do you think would happen to it if there was
no friction at all?

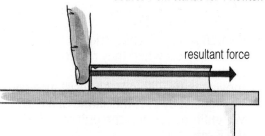

We show forces in diagrams by arrows.
The bigger the force, the longer the arrow.

▶ Look at the diagram. It shows a book being pushed
across a table.

e Which is the bigger force: the push of the finger or
the force of friction?

f Do you think the book is moving? Why?

g How big is the push force in newtons? (Use your ruler to
measure it.)

h How big is the friction force?

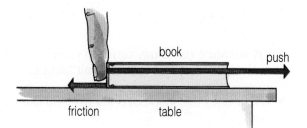

scale: 1 cm stands for 1 newton

The friction force cancels out part of the push force. We are left
with a **resultant** force.

i How big is the resultant force here?

j What would be the resultant force if the push force = 3 newtons
and the friction force = 2 newtons?

It is the resultant force that makes the book move.
The bigger the resultant force, the faster the book moves.

▶ Draw a diagram of the book and show a push force of
2 newtons and a friction force of 2 newtons.

k What is the resultant force?

l Does the book move or stay still?

Isaac Newton wrote a 'law' about these ideas:

If an object has **no** resultant force on it, then

● if it is at rest, it stays at rest (not moving)

● if it is moving, it keeps moving at a
steady speed in a straight line.

Investigating movement

Let a toy car roll down a slope:

Plan an investigation to see how the **time taken** by a car to travel down depends on the **height** it starts from.

You can use a pair of *light gates*: As the car passes through the first gate it starts an electrical timer. The timer stops as the car passes the second gate. The computer shows how long it took.

What do you think will happen? Write down your *prediction*.

- Make a list of things (variables) you will keep the same, to make it a fair test.
- How far apart will you place the light gates?
- Will you push the car or just let it go?
- How often will you repeat it at each height?
- How will you record your results?

Show your plan to your teacher and then do it.

What did you find out? Does it agree with your prediction?

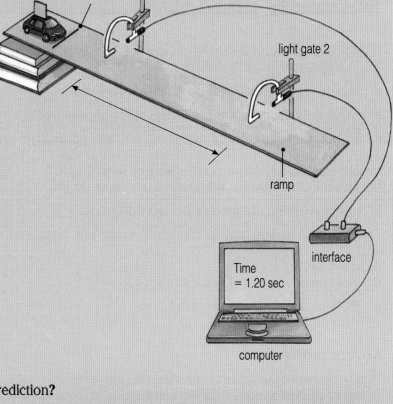

Now answer these questions. In your answers, try to include words from the box.

m Why does the car move down the ramp?

n Why does the car eventually stop moving?

o When the car has stopped, where has its energy gone to?

The diagram shows a car moving along a level road:

p Why is there a force shown acting backwards?

q If the car is moving at constant speed, how big is this force?

weight	**pull of gravity**
resultant force	**friction**
balanced forces	**air resistance**
potential energy	**kinetic energy**

push due to engine

2000 N

---

1 Copy and complete:
a) An object can have . . . . than one force acting on it.
b) If there is no resultant . . . . on the object, its movement does . . . . change.
c) Newton's law on this says: if an object has no . . . . force on it, then
 - if it is at rest then it stays at . . . . (not . . . .)
 - if it is moving then it keeps on . . . . at a . . . . speed in a . . . . line.

2 Use a scale of 1 cm for 1 newton to draw force diagrams for:
a) a book being pushed by a force of 6 N with a friction force of 2 N
b) a toy boat weighing 4 N floating on water (see the diagram on page 148).

3 Look at the children sliding on page 145. Describe in as much detail as you can,
a) the forces on them,
b) the energy changes, as they slide down.

Things to do

Speed on!

Learn about:
● speed and its units
● stopping distances
● distance – time graphs

Have you ever noticed the speed cameras at the side of some roads? You will find them at places where motorists tend to drive too fast.

a Where are speed cameras positioned in your area?

b What are your views on the benefits of speed cameras?

c Do you know the normal speed limit in a built-up area?

In your answer to **c**, did you use **miles per hour** (mph)? We also measure speed in **kilometres per hour** (km/h).

In Science we often use **metres per second** (m/s).

These units all tell you how far something travels in a given time.

A car is travelling at 15 m/s.
d How far does it go in 1 second?

e How far does it go in 4 seconds?

A speed camera

Safety matters

When a driver has to brake, it takes time for him to react. In that fraction of a second, the car can travel many metres. This is called the **thinking distance**.

People have different reaction times. For most people, when they are not expecting to brake, the reaction time is 0.7 second!

f Suppose you were driving at 20 m/s (this is 45 mph).
If your reaction time is 0.7 s, how far would you travel before you started to press the brake?

g How would this thinking distance be affected if the driver was tired?
What else could affect this thinking distance?

▶ The **braking distance** is the distance the car will travel *after* the brake is pressed.

h At 20 m/s (45 mph) on a dry road, with good brakes, the braking distance is 31 m. What is the **total stopping distance**?

i On a wet road, the braking distance is *twice* as much. **Why** is it longer?
What is the total stopping distance then?

j What other things would affect the braking distance?

No seat belts! Testing cars with dummies

Shortest stopping distances, *on a dry road, with good brakes*

At 13 m/s (*30 mph*)

Thinking distance	Braking distance	Total stopping distance
9 m	14 m	23 m

At 22 m/s (*50 mph*)

Thinking distance	Braking distance	Total stopping distance
15 m	38 m	53 m

At 30 m/s (*70 mph*)

Thinking distance	Braking distance	Total stopping distance
21 m	75 m	96 m

The distances shown in car lengths are based on an average family car.

Finding your reaction time

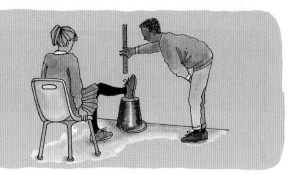

- You can find your reaction time by measuring how far a ruler falls before you can stop it. You can use your hand or a foot:

  Your teacher will give you a Help Sheet with a time scale for this. Your partner must release the ruler when you are not expecting it.

- Find your reaction time when you are thinking of something else. For example, talking to someone.

To see how speed varies during a journey, it helps to draw a graph.
It can show you where you speed up or slow down.

Distance – time graph

Imagine going on a bicycle ride.
The graph shows a bike ride with 3 parts, labelled **A**, **B**, **C**.
Look at the labels on the 2 axes:

Part **A**.
The cyclist is travelling at **a steady speed**. As **time** passes (along the graph), the **distance** increases (up the graph).

Part **B**.
The cyclist has **stopped** for a rest. As time passes (along the graph), the distance stays the same.

Part **C**.
The cyclist is now travelling again, and is going **faster** than before.
The graph is **steeper**, because she is travelling a bigger distance in each second.
The faster the speed, the steeper the slope or **gradient**.

k How would the graph be different if she had stayed for a longer rest in part B?

l How would it be different if she had moved even faster in part C?

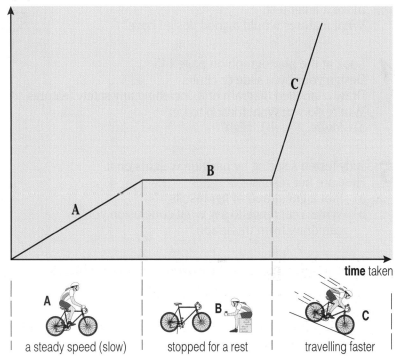

distance travelled by cyclist

time taken

A — a steady speed (slow) | B — stopped for a rest | C — travelling faster

---

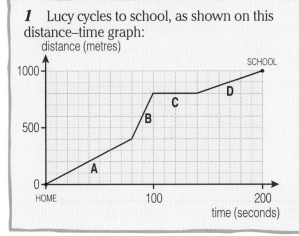

1 Lucy cycles to school, as shown on this distance–time graph:

distance (metres)

HOME

time (seconds)

a) Which parts show that Lucy is moving?
b) For how long did she stop at some traffic lights?
c) Which part is most likely to show her going down a hill? Explain why.
d) How far did she travel during part A?
e) Calculate her speed during part A.
f) Calculate her speed during part B.
g) How far is it from home to school?
h) Calculate her average speed for the whole journey.

2 Explain what is meant by **gradient**.

Things to do

Questions

1 Streamlining reduces friction.
Give 3 examples of streamlining in animals, and explain how it helps the animals.

2 How is friction reduced in:
a) a hovercraft?   b) a racing car?   c) a yacht?

3 Plan an investigation of a toy sailing boat.
Decide what you would investigate, and how you would make it a fair test.
What features would a good design have?

4 Look at the photograph on page 145.
Design your own slide or chute.
Draw a labelled diagram of it, including any safety features.
Where do you want friction to be:
a) low?   b) high?

5 Judy tested a spring by hanging weights on it.
Here are her results:
a) Plot a line-graph of her results.
b) Write a sentence to say what conclusion you can draw from this graph.

weight (N)	1	2	3	4	5	6
extension (mm)	15	30	45	60	80	120

6 Write a 'safety checklist' for **either** a pram **or** a bicycle.
It should show what you would check to see if it is safe to use.

7 The table tells you about the braking distances for a car going at 15 metres per second (33 m.p.h.):
a) Draw a bar-chart of the data, and label it.
b) What is the best combination of road and tyres for stopping quickly? What is the braking distance in this case?
c) What is the worst combination? How much worse is it than the best combination?
d) Why is it harder to stop on wet roads than on dry roads?

Braking distances		
Dry road	new tyres	13 metres
	old tyres	14 metres
Wet road	new tyres	18 metres
	old tyres	23 metres

8 Holly the cat goes for a little walk.
Here is her distance–time graph:

a) Use the scales on the graph to describe her journey in as much detail as you can.
b) What is her speed in part A?
c) Sketch the graph you would get if she runs twice as fast in parts A and C.
Add the correct numbers to your axes.

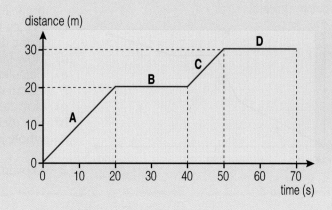

The Solar System and beyond

Here is a photo of our beautiful planet Earth.
It is one of the 9 planets that go round the Sun.

Our Sun is just one of the billions of stars in our galaxy.

And our galaxy is just one of the billions of galaxies in our Universe . . . .

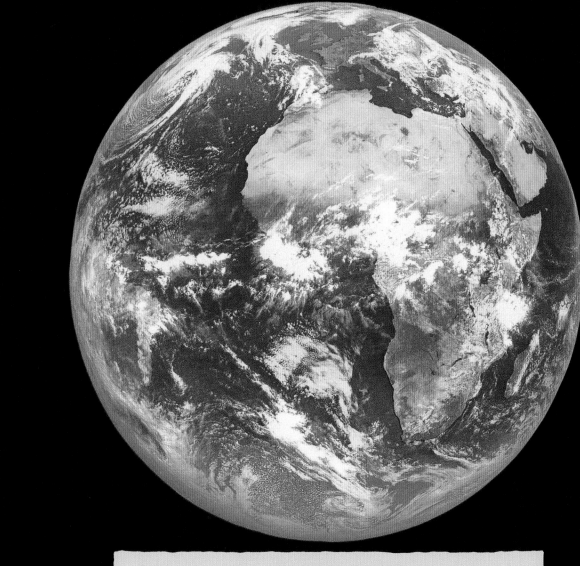

Earth and the Sun

Learn about:
● day and night
● a year and 4 seasons

Each morning, the Sun rises in the East.

a In which direction does it set at dusk?

b In which direction is it at mid-day?

c Why must you never look straight at the Sun?

d In winter, is the day-time shorter or longer than in summer?

e In winter, is the Sun higher or lower in the sky?

f What would happen on Earth if the Sun stopped shining?

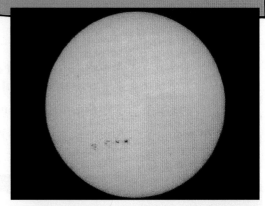

The Sun – our nearest star. On the same scale, the Earth is about the size of this full stop.

Day and night

Use a ball and a lamp (or a torch) to find out why we get day and night:

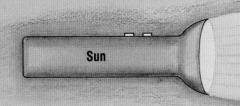

g If it is day-time for you, name a country where it is night-time.

h How many hours does it take for the Earth to spin round once?

i Which way does the Earth spin so that the Sun 'rises' in the East?

A year

Use a ball and a lamp to find out how the Earth moves in orbit round the Sun:

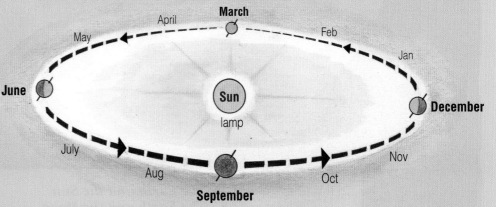

j How long does it take for the Earth to make one complete journey round the Sun?

k How many times does the Earth spin on its axis while it makes this journey?

l You are held on to the Earth by the force of gravity. What force do you think keeps the Earth in orbit round the Sun?

The 4 seasons

m Look at these 4 photos. Which season is shown in each one?

We have different seasons because the Earth's axis is **tilted**. The axis is tilted at $23\frac{1}{2}°$, like this:

As the Earth moves round the Sun, **it is always tilted the same way**, like this:

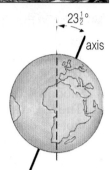

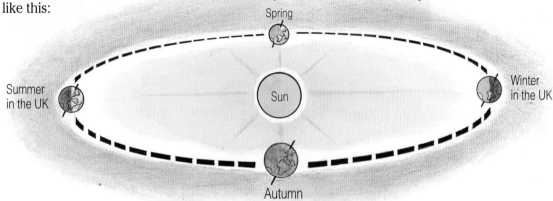

In summer, our part of the Earth is tilted towards the Sun.
The Sun appears to be higher in the sky, and daylight lasts longer.
So it is warmer.
In winter, our part of the Earth is tilted away from the Sun.
The Sun is lower in the sky, and the day-time is shorter. So it is colder.

Exploring your model Earth using ICT

Use the ball and lamp to show the 4 seasons. Mark your position on the ball, and watch it carefully as the Earth goes round the Sun. (Remember to keep the ball tilted in the same direction all the time.)

Place a **light sensor** in your position on the ball. Record the light intensity while you rotate the ball slowly (a) in its summer position, then (b) in its winter position.
n What do you notice about the length of daytime in each season?

Now place a **temperature sensor** on your tilted ball, at the North Pole in summer.
Move the sensor slowly straight down to the South Pole, monitoring the temperature.
o What do you notice about the change in temperature? How does this relate to the seasons?

1 Copy and complete:
a) A day is the time for the . . . . to . . . . once on its axis.
b) A year is the time it takes for the . . . . to travel once round the . . . .
c) In one year there are . . . . days.
d) The Earth's axis is tilted at an angle of . . . .
e) In summer, our part of the . . . . is tilted towards the . . . . , so the Sun appears . . . . in the sky and the days are . . . . and warmer.

2 A scarecrow, 1 metre high, is standing in the middle of a field. Write down as many things as you can about its shadow,
a) in summer, b) in winter.

3 How would our lives be different if:
a) The Earth was much closer to the Sun?
b) The Earth turned more slowly on its axis?
c) The Earth's axis was not tilted at all?

Things to do

Earth and the Moon

Learn about:
• the phases of the Moon
• lunar and solar eclipses

▶ Look at the photos:

a Write down 5 things that you know about the Moon.

b Would you like to live on the Moon? Why?

c The Moon shines at night, but it is not hot like the Sun. Where do you think the light comes from?

Full Moon　　　　An astronaut on the Moon

The Moon moves in an orbit round the Earth.
It is held in this orbit by the pull of gravity.
One complete orbit of the Moon takes about 1 month (1 'moonth').

The Moon looks different at different times of the month.
It has **phases**. A 'full moon' is one of the phases.

Phases of the Moon

Use a lamp and 2 balls to investigate the phases of the Moon:

The numbers 1–8 show 8 different positions of the Moon round the Earth. They are about 4 days apart.

At each position, look at the Moon from the position of the Earth. That is, from the **centre** of the circle.

On this diagram, some parts of the Moon are coloured yellow. These are the parts in sunlight that you can see from the Earth.

• Sketch what you see in each position when you are at the centre of the circle. Label your sketches with the correct names of the phases:

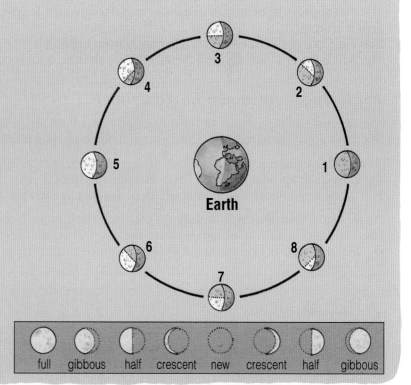

full　gibbous　half　crescent　new　crescent　half　gibbous

Observing the Moon

Your teacher will give you a Help Sheet on which you can record your observations of the Moon for the next month.

Eclipse of the Moon   (lunar eclipse)

When you stand in sunlight, there is a shadow behind you.
In the same way, there is a big shadow behind the Earth.
If the Moon moves into this shadow, we call it an **eclipse** of the Moon:

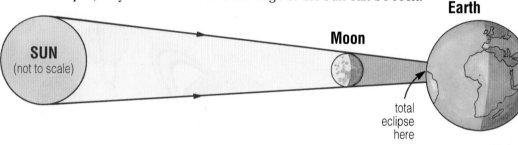

The Moon is not in the sunlight, and so it is dark.

Eclipse of the Sun   (solar eclipse)

This happens when the Moon comes directly between the Sun and the
Earth. Part of the Earth is in the Moon's shadow.
The sky goes dark even though it is day-time, because the Moon is
blocking out the Sun's rays.
In a total eclipse, only the flames round the edge of the Sun can be seen.

Total solar eclipse

Use a lamp and 2 balls to show:
1) an eclipse of the Moon, and   2) an eclipse of the Sun.

The Moon is covered in craters. We think they were caused by
large rocks from space, crashing into the Moon.
These rocks are called **meteorites**.

Design an investigation to find out what changes the **size and
shape of craters**. (Hint: you could use sand and marbles.)

Plan the investigation, and if you have time, do it.

---

1 Copy and complete:
a) The Moon takes one . . . . to go round
the . . . . In each position it looks
different to us, with different . . . .
b) In an eclipse of the Moon, the Moon
moves into the shadow of the . . . .
c) In an eclipse of the Sun, the . . . . blocks
out the light from the . . . . so that the
. . . . is in a shadow.

2 Design a Moon-station for an astronaut
to live in. Draw a plan and label all the
important features.

3 Draw a diagram of the Earth and Moon
to a scale of: 1 mm = 1000 miles.

Earth–Moon distance	=	240 000 miles
Earth's diameter	=	8000 miles
Moon's diameter	=	2000 miles

The Sun is 93 000 000 miles away, and
900 000 miles in diameter. Where would
the Sun be on your diagram?

4 Imagine watching a total eclipse of
the Sun with a crowd of people. Write a
newspaper article describing the event.

Things to do

The Solar System

Learn about:
- planets, moons, asteroids
- sizes of planets and the Sun
- scale of the Solar System

The Earth is a **planet**. It travels in an orbit round our star, the Sun.

a Which is bigger: the Sun or the Earth?
b How long does it take for the Earth to make 1 orbit of the Sun?

The Earth is one of a 'family' of 9 planets. All of them are orbiting round the Sun. This is the **Solar System**.

The 9 planets are different sizes:

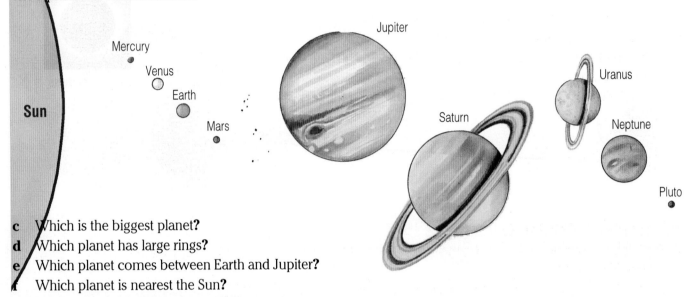

c Which is the biggest planet?
d Which planet has large rings?
e Which planet comes between Earth and Jupiter?
f Which planet is nearest the Sun?
g Which planet is farthest from the Sun?
h Which planet do you think will be the coldest?

Here are some data on the planets:

	Mercury	Venus	Earth	Mars	Asteroids	Jupiter	Saturn	Uranus	Neptune	Pluto
Diameter (km)	5000	12 000	12 800	7000	–	140 000	120 000	52 000	50 000	3000
Distance from the Sun (million km)	60	110	150	230	–	780	1400	2900	4500	6000
Time to travel 1 orbit round the Sun (years)	0.2	0.6	1	2	–	12	30	84	160	250

i Which planet is almost the same size as the Earth?

j Which planets are larger than the Earth?

k Which planet moves round the Sun in the shortest time?

l What pattern can you see between the **distance** from the Sun and the **time** taken for 1 orbit?

m What are the asteroids?

How far apart are the planets?

The distances between the planets are huge – much farther than the diagram on the opposite page shows.

Here is a scale diagram of the distances to the planets:

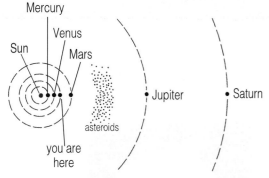

n Pluto is not shown on this diagram. Where would it be?

o Write down the names of the 4 inner planets.

p Why are these inner planets hotter than the 5 outer planets?

q Would the Sun look bigger or smaller from Mercury?

r Would the Sun look bright or dim from Pluto?

s What is the name of the force that holds the planets in orbit round the Sun?

t The orbit of each planet is not quite a circle. It is an **ellipse**. Draw an ellipse.

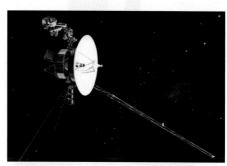

The Voyager-2 space probe

Make a scale model of the Solar System

1. For the Sun use a grapefruit or a cardboard disc with a diameter of 11 cm.

2. For the Earth make a small ball of plasticine just 1 mm across.
   Make all the other planets to the same scale, using the table below:

3. Hold your 'Earth' at a distance of 12 metres from your 'Sun'. Use the table to hold all the other planets at the correct distances.
   You will need to go on the playing field!

   On this scale the nearest star would be another grapefruit, about 3000 kilometres away!

	Mercury	Venus	Earth	Mars	Asteroids	Jupiter	Saturn	Uranus	Neptune	Pluto
Size of 'planet'	$\frac{1}{2}$ mm	1 mm	1 mm	$\frac{1}{2}$ mm		11 mm	9 mm	4 mm	4 mm	$\frac{1}{4}$ mm
Distance from 'Sun'	5 m	8 m	12 m	18 m		60 m	110 m	220 m	350 m	460 m

1 Copy and complete:

a) There are . . . . planets in the . . . . System.

b) The names of the 9 planets (in order) are:

c) The coldest planet is . . . . This is because it is the farthest from the . . . .

2 Why do you think Pluto was the last planet to be discovered?

3 Do you think it would be possible to live on Mercury? Explain your answer.

4 Plot a bar-chart of the diameters of the planets, using a spreadsheet if possible.

5 For the first 5 planets, plot a line-graph of the *time* taken to travel 1 orbit round the Sun against the *distance* from the Sun.

The asteroids are large rocks that travel round the Sun at an average distance of 400 million km. Use your graph to estimate how long they take to make 1 orbit.

Things to do

The planets

Learn about:
● conditions on the planets
● searching for patterns

▶ Use the information on these two pages to fill in a table like this one, or create a spreadsheet:

Planet	Type of surface	Average temperature	Type of atmosphere	Length of a 'day'	Moons, rings
Mercury					

Mercury is a small planet, about the size of our Moon. It has a rocky surface which is covered in craters.

It has no atmosphere. The side facing the Sun is very hot (about 430 °C, hot enough to melt lead).

Venus is almost as big as the Earth, but it is very unpleasant. Its rocky surface is covered by thick clouds of sulphuric acid.

The atmosphere is mainly carbon dioxide. This traps the Sun's heat (by the 'Greenhouse Effect') so that Venus is even hotter than Mercury.

From space, **Earth** is a blue planet with swirls of cloud. It is the only planet with water and oxygen and living things.

It is at the right distance from the Sun, with the right chemicals, to support life. Of course, other stars in the Universe may have planets with the same conditions.

Mars – the red planet – is a dry cold desert of red rocks, with huge mountains and canyons. No life has been found on Mars.

It has a thin atmosphere of carbon dioxide, and 2 small moons. Mars was the first of the planets to be visited by one of our space-craft.

Planet	Diameter (km)	Distance to Sun (million km)	Time for 1 orbit (planet's 'year')	Time for 1 spin (planet's 'day')	Average temperature on sunny side (°C)	Moons
Mercury	5000	60	88 days	1400 hours	+430	0
Venus	12 000	110	220 days	5800 hours	+470	0
Earth	12 800	150	$365\frac{1}{4}$ days	24 hours	+20	1
Mars	7000	230	2 years	25 hours	–20	2
Asteroids						
Jupiter	140 000	780	12 years	10 hours	–150	16
Saturn	120 000	1400	30 years	10 hours	–180	18 + rings
Uranus	52 000	2900	84 years	17 hours	–210	15 + rings
Neptune	50 000	4500	160 years	16 hours	–220	8
Pluto	3000	6000	250 years	150 hours	–230	1

Jupiter is the largest planet, and is very cold. It has no solid surface. It is mainly liquid hydrogen and helium, surrounded by these gases and clouds. The Giant Red Spot is a huge storm, 3 times the size of Earth. Jupiter has 16 moons.

Saturn is another 'gas giant', very like Jupiter. The beautiful rings are not solid. They are made of billions of chunks of ice and rock. They are held in orbit by the pull of Saturn's gravity.

Uranus is another 'gas giant', made of hydrogen and helium. Unlike the other planets it is lying on its side as it goes round the Sun. It was discovered in 1781 by William Herschel.

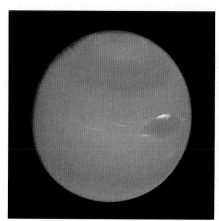

Neptune is very like Uranus. It is a blue 'gas giant'. The Great Dark Spot is a storm the size of Earth.

a Which planet is most like the Earth? Explain your reasons.

b Why is it hard for scientists to find out about i) Venus? ii) Pluto?

c Only one planet has liquid water on its surface. Why is this?

Pluto is the smallest planet, discovered in 1930. It is a rocky planet, covered in ice. It has a very thin atmosphere of methane.

▶ Search the data in your table or spreadsheet for any patterns.

What conclusions can you draw?
Explain how strong you think the evidence is for these conclusions.

Things to do

1 Imagine that you are an advertising agent for holidays in the year 2030. Choose one of the planets (not Earth) and:
a) make up an advertising slogan for it,
b) draw a poster or write a TV commercial for it.

2 Write a story about 'A journey through the Solar System'.

3 Explain why you think life developed on Earth and not on other planets.

4 Which planets have a thin atmosphere or none at all? Use your data to see if it has anything to do with size.
Can you think of a reason for this?

5 Write a brief account of the work of William Herschel and his sister, Caroline.

The Universe

Learn about:
- stars and galaxies
- the expanding Universe
- evidence for life

Our Sun is a **star**. It is like all the others you can see in the night sky. They are all **luminous**.
In size, the Sun is just an average star.

The star patterns you can see at night are called **constellations**.
For example, the Plough (or Great Bear) looks like this:

▶ Write down the names of any constellations that you know of. Your teacher may give you a star-map of the constellations.

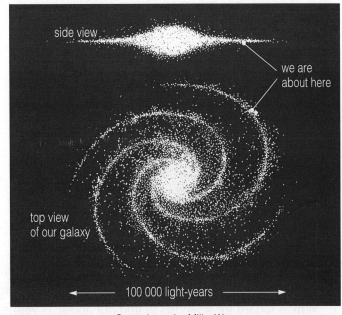

The Sun is part of a huge collection of stars called a **galaxy**. Our galaxy is called the Milky Way. It is a collection of more than 100 000 million stars!

Our galaxy has a *spiral* shape. We are in one of the spiral arms:

Our galaxy is huge. It takes light just 8 minutes to travel from the Sun to Earth, but it takes 100 000 years for light to travel across our galaxy!

A **light-year** is the *distance* that light travels in one year. And light travels at a speed of 300 000 kilometres per second!

Radio waves also travel at the speed of light.
Nothing can travel faster than this.

side view

we are about here

top view of our galaxy

← 100 000 light-years →

Our galaxy, the Milky Way

Other galaxies

The Milky Way is our galaxy, but it is not the only galaxy. It is one of a group of 20 galaxies called the **Local Group**.
The Andromeda galaxy is one of these:

Through telescopes we can see *millions* of other galaxies!
All the galaxies together, and the space between them, form the **Universe**.

Some galaxies are so far away that it has taken the light 10 000 million years to reach us. So we see them as they *were*, 10 000 million years ago!

So the universe is even older than this.

The Andromeda galaxy.
It contains 300 billion stars and is 2 million light-years away from us.

The expanding universe

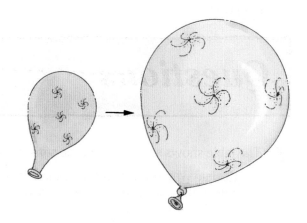

In 1929, Edwin Hubble discovered that the galaxies are moving apart. The universe is expanding!

This is rather like a balloon which has some ink-marks on it. The ink-marks represent the galaxies. The balloon is the universe. As the balloon is blown up, the universe expands and all the galaxies move farther apart.
This is a 'model' of our expanding universe.

Thinking back in time, the universe was once very small. Astronomers believe it started about 12 000 million years ago, in an explosion called the **Big Bang**.
It has been expanding ever since.

Your place in the universe

Your teacher will give you a Help Sheet for this.
Cut out the pictures and sort them into the right order.
This will show you how you fit into the universe.

- What is your full address in the universe?

Making a telescope

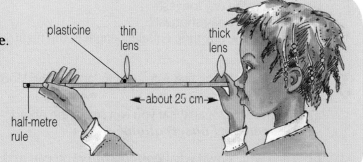

To look at the universe, an astronomer uses a **telescope**.

You can make a telescope by using 2 lenses, like this:

Look through the lenses, and move the thin lens along the ruler until you see a sharp image. (Never look at the Sun through a telescope).

- What do you notice about the image that you see?

ET . . . Extra-Terrestrial

Do you think there could be other life in the Universe? Perhaps on another planet in our Solar System, or a planet round another star?

What evidence would you look for in searching for life?

Suppose you were going to send a 'space-capsule' on a long journey into space. It may be found by aliens (who won't understand English). What would you put into the capsule to tell the aliens about yourself?

---

1 Copy and complete:
a) The Sun is really an ordinary . . . . It is part of our . . . . , called the Milky Way.
b) A light-year is the . . . . that light travels in one . . . .
c) The universe has been . . . . since the time of the . . . .

2 The speed of light is 300 000 km/s. How far, in kilometres, is a light-year?

3 Here is a list of objects:
star moon galaxy planet universe
a) Put them in order of size (smallest first).
b) For each one, write a sentence to explain what it is.

4 To travel to another star would take centuries. Sketch the design of a space-ship for this. What would be the problems for the people on board?

Things to do

Questions

1 The table shows some data for the sunshine in London:

a) Explain why summer is hotter than winter.
b) Sketch the path of the Sun through the sky for
   i) a day in January, and   ii) a day in July.

Month	Altitude of midday sun	Hours of daylight
January	low, 15°	8
July	high, 62°	16

2 The table shows the times of sunrise and sunset in London throughout the year:

Date	Jan 21	Feb 21	Mar 21	Apr 21	May 21	Jun 21	Jul 21	Aug 21	Sep 21	Oct 21	Nov 21	Dec 21
Sunrise	8.0	7.2	6.0	5.0	4.1	3.7	4.1	4.8	5.8	6.6	7.4	8.1
Sunset	16.3	17.3	18.2	19.1	19.8	20.3	20.1	19.3	18.1	17.0	16.1	16.0

(All the times are in decimal hours and GMT on a 24-hour clock)

a) On graph paper, plot the sunrise times against the date.
   Then plot the sunset times on the same diagram.
b) When is the day longest?
c) When is the day shortest?
d) When is the day-time equal in length to the night?

3 The photo shows the first astronaut to land on the Moon:

a) Describe first of all what you can see in the photo.
   These are your **observations**.

b) Then write down what **conclusions** you can make from:
   i)   his clothes,
   ii) his shadow,
   iii) the black sky,
   iv) his foot-marks,
   v)   his small space-craft,
   vi) the label under the photograph.

Neil Armstrong, 1969

4 Some pupils are thinking and hypothesizing:

Ayesha says, "I think that the farther a planet is from the Sun, the cooler it is."
Danielle says, "I think that the larger a planet is, the more moons it has."
Chris says, "I think that the farther a planet is from the Sun, the longer the time for 1 orbit (the planet's 'year')."

Do the data in the table on page 166 support any of these hypotheses? Explain your thinking. If you can, draw graphs to show how the data agree with the hypotheses.

5 Using a book, a ROM or the internet, write a paragraph about each of these:
a) a supernova,   b) a neutron star (pulsar),   c) a black hole,   d) a quasar.

6 In 1670, Blaise Pascal, a French scientist, wrote "Le silence éternel de ces espaces infinis m'effraie" (*The eternal silence of these infinite spaces terrifies me*).
Write a poem of your thoughts about space.

7M

In Science we look for ways to investigate our world.
We do this by observing and measuring, and looking for evidence.
Then we try to find patterns in this evidence, by interpreting and concluding.
We also make predictions, which we can test, making sure that we evaluate our evidence carefully.

In this unit we look at these skills in more detail.

In this unit:

Measuring

In science, just observing with your eyes may not be accurate enough. You often need to **measure** things.

▶ For example, look at these two black lines: which *looks* longer, A or B?
To be sure, you need to measure each line accurately, with a ruler. Which is longer, A or B?
What is the length of each, in mm?

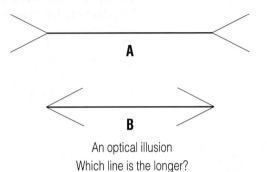

An optical illusion
Which line is the longer?

In this lesson you are going to use thermometers, clocks and measuring cylinders. Each of these instruments has a *scale* with marks on it. You should always measure carefully on the scale, to the *nearest mark*.

Using a measuring cylinder

This measures in units called **centimetres-cubed**, written **cm³**.

Look at the scale on a measuring cylinder or jug.
What is the maximum (biggest) **volume** it can measure?

Count the number of divisions between two of the numbers on the scale. How big is *one* division (in cm³)?

Pour in some water, until it is about half-full.
Then take the reading, making sure that:
● the measuring cylinder is *vertical*, not sloping
● your eye is *level* with the bottom of the water surface.
What is the volume of the water?

Practise reading the scale with different amounts of water.
Check your partner's readings.

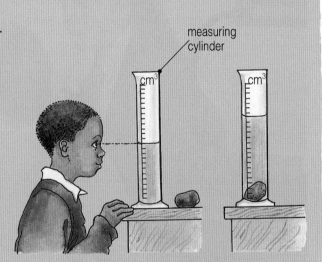

measuring cylinder

If you have time …

Finding the volume of a pebble

Now gently drop in a pebble (or another object that sinks in water).
Why does the water level rise?

What is the volume reading now? (This is the volume of the water *and* the pebble.)

How can you work out the volume of the pebble?
What is the volume of the pebble, in cm³?

Try again with a different amount of water.
Do you get the same result? Try it a third time.

What is the advantage of *repeating* results like this?

	Volume of water (cm³)	Volume of water + pebble (cm³)	∴ Volume of pebble (cm³)
1			
2			
3			
		Average =	

Using a thermometer

This measures in units called **degrees Celsius**, written **°C**.

Look at the scale on the thermometer. What is the maximum (highest) **temperature** it can measure? What is the minimum?

Look at the smallest divisions on the scale. How big is one of these divisions (in °C)?

What is the temperature of the thermometer now?
What happens if you warm the bulb end gently with your hand?
Can you explain this?

Now use a measuring cylinder (see the opposite page) to measure 100 cm³ of water into a beaker.
Copy out the table ready for your results.
Take the temperature of the water. Record it on the first line of your table.

Put the beaker on a tripod. Light a Bunsen burner and start heating the water. Stir the water gently and take its temperature every minute, for 8 minutes.

⚠

Leave the beaker and tripod to cool before moving them!
Look at the results in your table. Is there a pattern?

How would your results be different if you used:
- more water?
- a smaller flame?

If you have time, plot a line-graph of your results, with **time** along the bottom and **temperature** up the side.

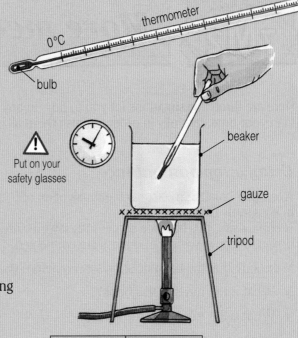

Time (minutes)	Temperature (°C)
0	
1	
2	
3	
4	
5	
6	
7	
8	

Things to do

1 Study the diagrams. What is the reading at each of the arrows (a to m)? (Remember: you always read to the nearest mark.)

2 Make a list of 5 measuring instruments used in your home.

3 If you have a measuring jug and a marker pen, how could you use bath-time to find the volume of your body?

4 A pack of 500 sheets of paper is 50 mm thick. How thick is one sheet?

5 A problem: you need to find the volume of a stone but it is too large to fit into your measuring cylinder. It will fit into a beaker, and you have enough water to fill the beaker. How can you find the volume of the stone?

6 Which of these cylinders would you use to find the volume of a small button? Why?

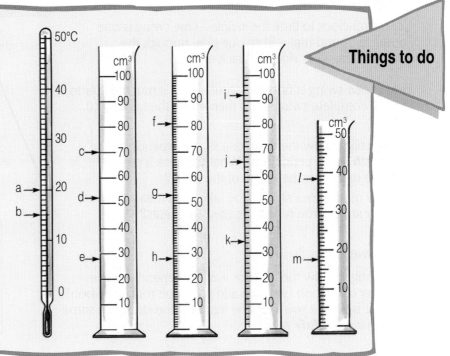

More measuring

Learn about:
- measuring mass
- measuring time
- using a pulse monitor

Here are three investigations for you to do – in any order.
Plan your time carefully in order to finish them all.

Using a top-pan balance

A top-pan balance measures the **mass** of an object, in grams (**g**) or in kilograms (**kg**).
(People using this balance sometimes say they are 'weighing' an object, because weight and mass are connected, see page 152.)

Make sure that the balance shows **zero** before you start.

- What is the mass of this book?

- What is the mass of a 10p coin?

- Estimate the mass of a 20p coin, and then measure it.

- What is the mass of one paper-clip?
  If you have 20 identical paper-clips, how can you find the mass of one paper-clip more accurately?

- How can you find the mass of 100 cm³ of water?

top-pan balance

Finding the mass of 1 pin

mass of 100 pins = 10.0 g

$$\text{average mass of 1 pin} = \frac{10.0}{100} = 0.1 \text{ g}$$

Investigating a pendulum

You can make a pendulum from a piece of string with a weight or 'bob' at the end of it.

Use a stop-clock to time the swings. One swing is one complete 'round-trip' – from one side, through the middle to the other side and back again.

Timing one swing is not very accurate – it is much better to time 10 complete swings, and then divide the time by 10.

- Investigate how the time for a swing depends on the **length** of the pendulum. What happens if you halve or double the length of the string?

  How many times should you take each measurement?
  Why should you repeat the measurements?

If you have time ...

- Investigate how the time for a swing depends on the **mass** of the bob (you can add plasticine round the bob). Make sure that you keep the length of the string the same so that it is a **fair test**.

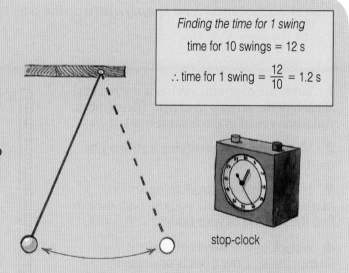

stop-clock

Finding the time for 1 swing

time for 10 swings = 12 s

$$\therefore \text{ time for 1 swing} = \frac{12}{10} = 1.2 \text{ s}$$

Length (cm)	Time for 10 swings (seconds)	Time for 1 swing (seconds)

Measuring your body

Everyone's body is different – and we each have different measurements.

Make these measurements and keep a record of them:

- your height (in cm)

- the length from your elbow to the tip of your middle finger (in cm). This length used to be called your 'cubit'.

- your mass (in kg)

- the temperature of your armpit (in °C)

- your normal breathing rate (breaths per minute)

- your normal pulse rate (beats per minute or 'bpm')

A **pulse monitor** can be used to measure your pulse rate. Attach the sensor to your body, and connect it to a computer:

Record your normal pulse for 2 minutes.
What is the average?

Run on the spot for 1 minute.
Then record your pulse rate… until it returns to normal.

How long does it take for your pulse rate to return to normal?
This is a measure of your fitness.

Plot a graph of your **pulse rate** against **time**.
In your group, compare the graphs. Can you see a pattern?

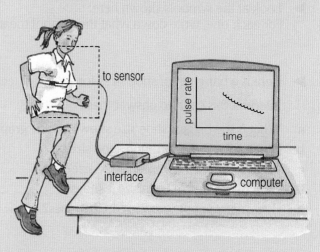

Measuring your pulse rate

Things to do

1 Take your pulse several times each day for the next 3 days. Does it vary?
When is it highest? When is it lowest?

2 Why is it more accurate to time 10 swings of a pendulum rather than just one swing?

3 Noah built his Ark boat to be 300 cubits long. How long is your cubit? How long would the Ark have been if you had built it? Why is a cubit not used today?

4 An empty beaker 'weighs' 50 grams. When it contains 100 cm³ of water, it 'weighs' 150 g. What is the mass of 100 cm³ of water?

5 50 nails have a mass of 200 grams. What is the average mass of one nail? Why have we used the word 'average' here?

6 A measuring cylinder contains 20 cm³ of water. When 4 marbles are put in the water, the reading becomes 32 cm³.
What is the average volume of a marble?

7 An Italian boy called Galileo was the first person to notice that a pendulum swings with a constant time for each swing.

Research, using an encyclopedia (a book or a ROM) or the internet, to find out:
a) When did Galileo live?
b) What else is he famous for?

Galileo as an old man

Interpreting and concluding

We have looked at the skills of observing and measuring. In this lesson we are looking at another skill: **interpreting**. Interpreting means making sense of information or *data*.

In science you need to interpret information that is shown in different ways. It may be in tables or on graphs. Or it may be in symbols.

1	2	3	4
In this book	A road sign	On clothes	On a camera

5	6	7	8
On paper	On a bottle	On a bottle	In this book

▶ Look at the symbols shown here:
For each one, write down what the symbol means.

▶ Here is a bar-chart of shoe sizes for a class of teenagers.

Interpret this chart to answer these questions:

a What is the biggest shoe size shown on the graph?

b What is the most common shoe size?

c What is the least common shoe size?

d How many people have size 4 shoes?

e How many people are there in this class?

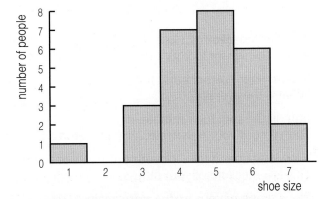

Look around the room and count the number of people you think have 'light' hair, 'dark' hair or 'red' hair.

Draw a bar-chart of your information. Label your chart.

Other people's charts may be different. Why is this?

▶ The table below shows some data on stereo radio recorders.

Interpret this information to answer these questions:

f Which is the cheapest?

g Which is the one that has a tone control?

h Which one does not have a built-in microphone?

i Which one would you buy if you had £80 to spend?
Explain your reasons.

Key:
B = Built-in microphone   A = Autostop of tape
H = Headphone socket   R = autoReverse to
T = Tone control   play second side

Make	From	Price (£)	Size (cm)	Weight (kg)	General features	Cassette features	No. of decks	Cassette battery running costs
Realistic SCR90	Hong Kong	40	13 × 35 × 8	1.5	B	A	1	6p per hour
Sony CFS903L	Taiwan	80	20 × 44 × 13	2.6	B H T	A R	1	12p per hour
JVC RC-W210	Malaysia	80	16 × 62 × 17	4.9	H	A	2	10p per hour
Philips AW7392	Austria	70	15 × 50 × 14	3.0	B H	A R	2	6p per hour

▶ Chris put a Bunsen burner under a beaker of water for a few minutes, and then took it away.

She plotted a line-graph of temperature against time, as shown here:

She has drawn a 'line of best fit' through the crosses.

Look at the graph, and interpret it and '***draw conclusions***' to answer these questions:

j How can you tell that the water got hotter**?**

k What was the temperature of the water at the start**?**

l What was the temperature after 2 minutes**?**

m How long did it take to reach 60 °C**?**

n What was the highest temperature**?**

o What was the rise in temperature of the water**?**

p Which result do you think is wrong**?**

q What do you think this result should be**?** Why**?**

r For how many minutes do you think the Bunsen burner was under the beaker before she took it away**?**

s Imagine Chris had put more water in the beaker. Sketch the graph that you would expect. Explain why.

t Why is a line-graph better than a bar-chart here**?**

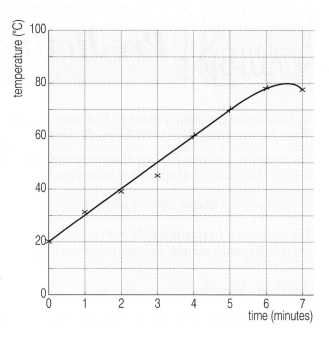

▶ Here is a photo of a sundial.

Your task is to ***interpret*** this photo by drawing up two lists:

Things that I can see on the photo. These are my ***observations***.	Things that I can work out or ***conclude*** from the photo. These are my ***conclusions***.
I can see a shadow. I can see a...	It is day-time. The sun is shining. I can tell that...

A sundial

1 In a survey of 30 pupils, 15 said that smoking should be banned, 10 said it shouldn't, and the rest didn't know.
From these data:
a) plot a bar-chart
b) plot a pie-chart.
Which chart do you prefer? Why?

2 Alan's answer to question **r** above was "The Bunsen burner was under the beaker for exactly 6 minutes". Emma disagreed. She said, "You can't be sure it was exactly 6 minutes". Who do you think was right? Justify and explain your answer.

3 Use the data below to plot a line-graph of temperature against time, like the one shown at the top of this page.

Time (minutes)	0	1	2	3	4	5
Temperature (°C)	10	30	45	55	60	62

Use your graph to find the temperature after $3\frac{1}{2}$ minutes.

4 Jessica heated some water with a Bunsen. Use a graph to decide which of her results may be wrong. What do you think they should be?

Time (minutes)	0	1	2	3	4	5	6
Temperature (°C)	15	26	41	48	59	67	81

Things to do

Predicting and Evaluating

In Science we are always trying to find ideas to explain our world. Then we use these ideas to make predictions.

For example, Lee was looking at some water that had spilled on the bench. The water was spreading across the bench. He said,

"I think water *always* flows downwards."

His idea was a **hypothesis** (*hi-poth-e-sis*).
He was **hypothesizing** (*hi-poth-e-size-ing*).

Anju had a better hypothesis. She said,

"I think water *always* flows downhill **because** gravity pulls it down."

These ideas are **hypotheses** (*hi-poth-e-sees*).
A hypothesis is a general idea about things which always happen.

A **prediction** is what you think will happen in a particular case.

From these hypotheses Pat made a **prediction**: "If you go to Egypt, you'll find the River Nile is flowing downhill."

The River Nile

▶ In your group, discuss these 3 boxes. Write down a hypothesis for each one. Start your sentence with 'I think' and include the word '*always*'. Then also try to include the word '*because*'.

Hypotheses have to be tested, to see if they are true. We can do this by:
• making a prediction,
• collecting evidence, and then
• seeing if the evidence supports the prediction.

▶ Look at this cartoon. Sarah is testing a hypothesis:

| 1 | When you were observing a candle flame and a Bunsen flame, you saw that they both point upwards. |

| 2 | Milk lasts longer if you put it in a fridge. |

| 3 | If you leave an ice-cube on the bench, it turns to water. Why is this? |

Hypothesizing

A torch will always work well when it has new batteries.

Predicting

My torch is not working. It will work if I put in new batteries.

Looking at the evidence

Drat! It is still not working. My hypothesis must be wrong.

Evaluating the evidence

Jack and Sophie made a prediction:

"We think that the roaring flame of a Bunsen burner will be hotter than its normal flame." (see page 7)

Then they looked for evidence, like this:

Then they did the same again, two more times. Their results are shown here:

This was their conclusion:

"The roaring flame is hotter because the temperature went higher when we used the roaring flame."

	Temperature with the normal flame (°C)	Temperature with the roaring flame (°C)
1	27	28
2	22	28
3	29	29

Look at the details of their work carefully, and then answer these questions to **evaluate** it.

a Look at their conclusion. Do you think they have enough evidence to support their conclusion? Explain your answer.

b Look at their table. One of their results looks wrong ('anomalous'). Which one? Can you explain what might have happened?

c Safety is important. Do you think that Jack and Sophie were working safely? Explain your answer.

d Look at the way they did the investigation.
Find as many mistakes as you can, and list them. (Five?)
Then explain in detail how they could improve their investigation.

---

1 People usually hang out their washing to dry on a warm dry day.

Write down your **hypothesis** about this, using the word '**always**'.
Now make your sentence longer, using the word '**because**'.
Then write down a **prediction** you can make from your hypothesis.
How could you test your hypothesis?

2 Tom says, "*I think warm water always evaporates faster than cold water.*"
Use this hypothesis to write a prediction.
Then explain carefully how you could collect evidence to test your prediction.

3 Chloe says, "*I think metal objects can always be picked up by magnets.*"
Do you think she is right?
Use her hypothesis to write a prediction.
Then explain how you could collect enough evidence to test this prediction.

Things to do

7M5 Planning a fair test

Learn about:
- variables
- planning a fair test

In Science you often have to **plan** an investigation.

An important part of your plan is to decide what you are going to change or *vary*. The things that you vary are called **variables**.

Variables

These are all the things that can change or vary during your investigation. They are sometimes called *factors*.

In your plan you will:

- *decide which thing should change.*
  This is the variable that you will change in the test.
  It is called the **independent** (or **input**) variable.

- *decide which thing you will judge or measure.*
  This variable changes as a result of varying the independent variable. It is called the **dependent** (or **outcome**) variable.

- *decide which things must not change.*
  These are the things you must keep the same, to make it a *fair test*. These are called **control** variables.

Here is an example to explain this.

Variables are things that vary and change.

Suppose you had to carry out an investigation with the title:
'How does the amount of water given to a plant affect its growth?'

You could do this investigation by planting seeds in several pots. Then you could give each plant a different amount of water each day. You would measure the height of the plant each day.

The amount of water that you give to each plant is one of the variables. You could measure this variable with a measuring jug. This is the **independent** (or **input**) variable.

The height of the plant is another variable. You would measure this variable with a ruler. This is the **dependent** (or **outcome**) variable.

It is important that the investigation is a **fair test**.

To make it a fair test, you have to *control* any other factors.
To control the other factors you would:
- use the *same* seeds in all the pots
- use the *same* soil in all the pots
- use the *same* size pots
- put the pots in the *same* position in the room.
These are the **control** variables.

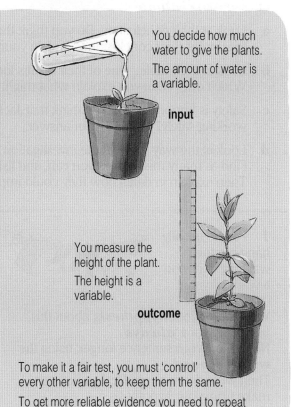

You decide how much water to give the plants.
The amount of water is a variable.

input

You measure the height of the plant.
The height is a variable.

outcome

To make it a fair test, you must 'control' every other variable, to keep them the same.

To get more reliable evidence you need to repeat this with many plants, to increase the **sample size**.

In the boxes below are three investigations for you to plan.

Investigation 1

How does the **height** that a ball bounces depend upon the **surface** that it bounces on?

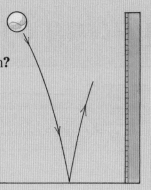

Plan:

What are you going to change?

What are you going to measure?

What are you going to keep the same (to make it a fair test)?

What can you do to make your results more reliable?   Make a table for your results.

What kind of graph could you use to show your results?

Investigation 2

How does the **length** of an elastic band depend upon the **weights** hanging from it?

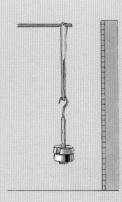

Plan:

What are you going to change?

What are you going to measure?

What are you going to keep the same (to make it a fair test)?

Make a table for your results.

What kind of graph could you use to show your results? Sketch what you think it will look like.

Investigation 3

How does your **pulse rate** depend upon the **amount of exercise** you do?

Plan:

What are you going to change?

What are you going to measure?

What are you going to control (to make it a fair test)?

Make a table for your results.

What kind of graph could you use to show your results?
Sketch what you think it will look like.

▶ If you have time, do one of these investigations.

Things to do

1 Look again at Investigation 1 above.
a) It will not be easy to measure the height that the ball bounces. Explain how taking the results 3 times at each height can make the evidence more reliable.
b) Here are 5 surfaces that a ball could bounce on:
carpet, concrete, wood, bed, grass.
Predict the order of what you think will be the highest to lowest bounce.
c) Then try it. Did you predict correctly?

2 Look again at Investigation 2.
a) Where would you put the zero mark of the ruler?
b) Scientists usually take at least 5 results in order to draw a line-graph. Explain why you think this is a good idea.

3 Look ahead to the next page, on Investigating. Read the left-hand page, and then choose one of the investigations. Plan it in detail so you are ready for the next lesson.

7M6 Investigating by a fair test

In the last few lessons you have used several skills for doing science:

- **P**redicting
- **P**lanning an investigation
- **O**bserving
- **M**easuring
- **I**nterpreting and drawing conclusions
- **C**ommunicating your results
- **E**valuating.

The diagram shows how they link together for a fair test.

Sometimes the results of one investigation suggest a start for another investigation.

Start here

What are we investigating?
What do we think (predict) will happen?
Why do we think this will happen?

Predicting

How can we make it **a fair test**?
- what are we going to change?
- what are we going to measure?
- what are we going to keep the same?

Has our teacher checked it is safe?

Planning

What equipment do we need?
How are we going to use it?
How many readings do we take?

Observing and Measuring

Evaluating

Is our evidence good?
How could we improve the investigation?
Have we got an idea for another investigation?

How can we record our results?
- in a table?   • then a graph?
Is there a pattern in our results?
Does it fit our prediction?
Can we explain the pattern?
How reliable are our results?

Interpreting and Concluding

On the opposite page are suggestions for 3 investigations.

▶ Read them carefully. Then choose **one** of them (one that you haven't done before).

▶ Then **plan** it in detail (using this diagram). When your teacher has checked your plan, go ahead and do the investigation.

How can we tell other people about our investigation?
- in a report? (with a diagram?)
- on a poster?
- in a talk or in discussion?

Communicating

1. Getting soaked

Paper towels are often used in kitchens and washrooms.
What do you think makes a **good** paper towel?

You will be given samples of 3 different paper towels,
labelled **A**, **B** and **C**.

*Your job is to find out which of the towels is best at
soaking up water.*

Which towel would you recommend to a friend?

2. Tearing tissues

Television adverts for paper tissues often claim that they are
'strong even when wet'.
What do you think about this claim?

You will be given samples of 3 different makes of paper tissues,
labelled **X**, **Y** and **Z**.

*Your job is to find out which of these tissues is
strongest when wet.*

Which tissue would you recommend to a friend?

3. Flaming Bunsens

Ben and Liz are arguing about Bunsen burners.

Ben says, "A burner with its air-hole fully open is always faster at
heating up water than two burners with their holes half-open."

Liz disagrees, "Two burners are always faster because they use up
more gas."

What do you think?

How can you find out safely?

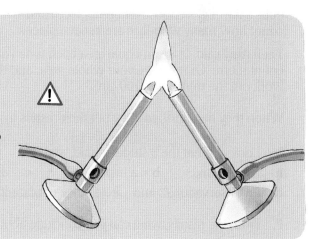

---

1 When you have done your investigation
think about how you could make it better.
You are **evaluating** it.
Write down your ideas (and draw diagrams
if they will help to explain).

2 Choose one of the other investigations
(one that you haven't done before).
Plan it in detail.

Things to do

Other ways of investigating

As well as 'fair test' investigations, there are other ways of doing a scientific enquiry.   As a scientist, you can:

- Collect data from books, ROMs or the internet.
- Identify and classify living things, rocks or chemicals.
- Study how things change over time: the Moon or a baby.
- Use models, simulations and analogies to explore ideas.
- Collect data about things that happen around us, and then **look for patterns** to explain them.

Looking for patterns

In these enquiries you have all sorts of natural variables. You cannot control them, so you cannot do a fair-test investigation. But you can still use your investigative skills.

Woodlice in the wild

Amy, Luke and Calum are in the garden, looking at woodlice, as you can see in the picture:

Amy said, "They are not under this dry stone."
Luke said, "Perhaps they like to be out in the open."

Calum wanted to investigate.
He said, "I think that we will find more under wet things than under dry things or out in the open."

Luke said, "Let's choose different places and count how many woodlice are in each place."

Then Amy said, "Use an equal area each time you count them. Or measure your whole area, and then work out the number in 100 cm^2."

Look at these woodlice under the pot.

Where do you think woodlice like to be?

I think they are always underneath things in the garden.

When they had finished, they put their results in a table:

▶ Look at what the 3 students said, and find:
a a question, **b** a hypothesis, **c** a prediction,
d an observation, and **e** a piece of planning.

f From the results, what can you conclude about where woodlice like to be?

g Does the evidence match Calum's hypothesis and his prediction?

h Make a prediction about what woodlice do when they are out in the light.

i Luke wrote this evaluation. What do you think is good (or bad) about it?

Place	Number of woodlice per 100 cm^2
Under a wet stone	69
Under bark of a dead tree	47
On a path	4
Under a smooth dry stone	0
Under wet leaves on soil	29
Amongst grass	5
Under a flower pot	32

There are some things we could not control: the wetness of the wet places, the temperature, other animals.
I think we can trust our conclusion because there was a big difference in the numbers we found in the wet and dry places.   We could look in more places. We could look for different kinds of woodlice in different places.

Charles Darwin was a scientist.
In 1831 he went on a voyage:

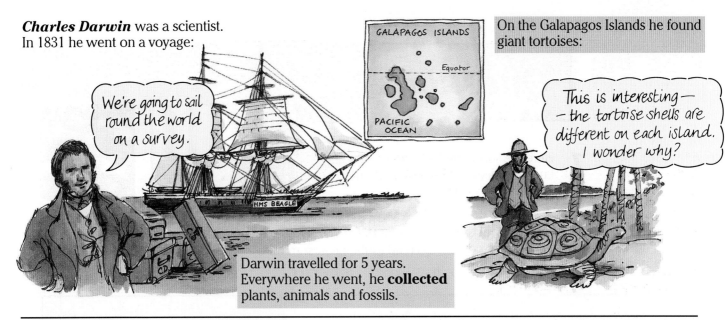

GALAPAGOS ISLANDS

Equator

PACIFIC OCEAN

We're going to sail round the world on a survey.

HMS BEAGLE

Darwin travelled for 5 years.
Everywhere he went, he **collected** plants, animals and fossils.

On the Galapagos Islands he found giant tortoises:

This is interesting — the tortoise shells are different on each island. I wonder why?

Charles **observed**, and looked for **patterns**.
He found that each island had its own species of finches (a bird).
There were 13 species of finches, and …

…. each has a different beak!

Charles looked for more **evidence** and found a **pattern**.
He found each species of finch ate a different food.

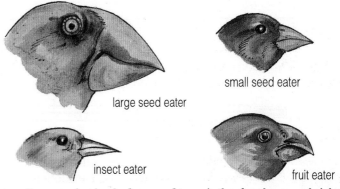

large seed eater

small seed eater

insect eater

fruit eater

Perhaps the species had **changed** to suit the food on each island**?**

He found lots more **evidence** on his voyage.
Back home, Darwin worked for 20 years
to **draw conclusions**.

I think all the species have changed, over a very long time.
They change to suit their environment.

… and the human species has changed as well.

Darwin and another scientist, Alfred Wallace, announced their 'Theory of Evolution' in 1858.

Darwin wrote a famous book:

The Origin of Species 1859

People were shocked at these new ideas.
Nowadays we have much more evidence, and most people believe Darwin was right.

---

1 In the story above, some words are emphasised: *collected, observed, pattern, evidence, draw conclusions.*
Explain what each one means, and why it is important in an investigation.

2 Use a book, a ROM or the internet to:
a) Find out more about Darwin's life, *or*
b) Find out more about his book, *or*
c) Find out why "People were shocked at these new ideas."

Things to do

Questions

1 Here are some mystery photos of well-known objects. Write down the name of each object.

2 What is the reading at each of the arrows (**a** to **o**)?
Remember: you always read to the nearest mark.

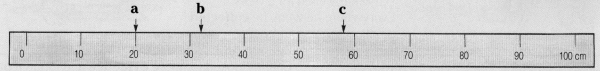

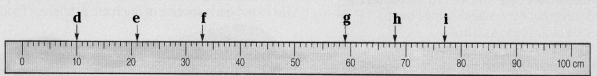

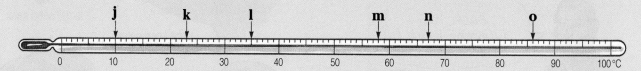

3 Which looks longer – the height of the hat or the width of the brim?
Which is longer? Give evidence to support your answer.

4 Lisa heated some water steadily with a Bunsen burner.

Her results are shown in the table:

a) On graph paper, draw two lines as axes.

Label the one along the bottom with **time** and mark the scale from 0 to 10 minutes.

Label the axis up the side with **temperature** and mark the scale from 0 °C to 100 °C.

b) Plot the 9 points on the graph, using small accurate crosses.

c) One of the results seems wrong. Which do you think it is?

d) Draw a straight 'line of best fit' through the other 8 points.

e) Use your graph to predict what the reading would be after 9 minutes.

f) If Lisa had used more water in her beaker, what would be different about the graph?

Time (minutes)	Temperature (°C)
0	20
1	25
2	30
3	40
4	40
5	45
6	50
7	55
8	60

5 Jason did the bouncing ball experiment shown on page 181.

a) Copy and complete this table of his results:

b) How reliable do you think his results are?

c) What conclusions can you draw from these results?

Ball dropped from a height of 100 cm

Surface	Height of bounce (in cm)			
	1st try	2nd try	3rd try	average
concrete	40	40	40	
carpet	20	24	22	
wood	27	29	28	
grass	21	36	9	

Glossary

Acid
A sour substance which can attack metal, clothing or skin. The chemical opposite of an alkali. When an acid is dissolved in water its solution has a pH number less than 7.

Adaptation
A feature that helps a plant or an animal to survive in changing conditions.

Adolescence
The time of change from a child to an adult, when both our bodies and our emotions change.

Alkali
The chemical opposite of an acid. Its solution has a pH number more than 7.

Amphibian
An animal that lives on land and in water. It has moist skin and breeds in water.

Asteroids
Small planets and pieces of rock hurtling through space. There is a belt of asteroids between Mars and Jupiter in the Solar System.

Balanced forces
Forces are balanced when they cancel out each other (see page 148). The object stays still, or continues to move at a steady speed in a straight line.

Biomass fuel
Fuel (e.g. wood) made from growing plants.

Boiling point
The temperature at which a liquid boils and changes into a gas.

Braking distance
The distance a car travels *after* the brake is pressed.

Carnivores
Animals that eat only other animals – meat-eaters.

Cell membrane
The structure that surrounds a cell and controls what goes in and out.

Cell wall
The strong layer on the outside of a plant cell that supports the cell.

Cells
The 'building blocks' of life, made up of a *cell membrane*, *cytoplasm* and *nucleus*.

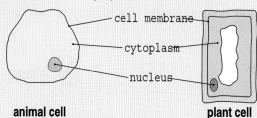

animal cell   plant cell

Chemical change
A change which makes a new substance, e.g. coal burning.

Chloroplasts
Tiny, round structures found inside plant cells. They capture light energy and use it to make food in photosynthesis.

Chromatography
A method used to separate mixtures of substances, usually coloured ones.

Combustion
The reaction which occurs when a substance burns in oxygen, giving out heat energy.

Component
One of the parts that make up an electric circuit, e.g. battery, switch, bulb.

Conductor
An electrical conductor allows a current to flow through it. A thermal conductor allows heat energy to pass through it. All metals are good conductors.

Control variables
The factors we must keep the same during an investigation to make sure we carry out a fair test.

Correlation
The strength of the link or connection between two variables being investigated.

Corrosive
A corrosive substance can eat away another substance by attacking it chemically.

Cytoplasm
The jelly-like part of the cell where many chemical reactions take place.

Dependent variable (or outcome variable)
When you do a fair test, this is the factor that you measure or observe in each test, in order to see the effect of varying another factor.

Diffusion
The process of particles moving and mixing of their own accord, without being stirred or shaken.

Distillation
A way to separate a liquid from a mixture of liquids, by boiling off the substances at different temperatures.

Drag
Friction caused by an object travelling through a liquid or gas. For example, friction caused by air resistance.

Eclipse
A *lunar eclipse* is when the shadow of the Earth falls on the Moon.

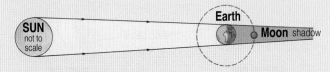

A *solar eclipse* is when the Sun is blotted out (totally or partially) by the Moon.

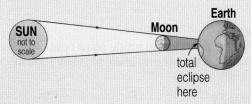

Ecosystem
A group of animals and plants plus the habitat in which they are found.

Egg
Female sex cell.

Electric current
A flow of electric charges (electrons).
It is measured in amps (A) by an ammeter.

Embryo
A fertilised egg grows into an embryo and eventually into a baby.

Evaluate
a) Your method,
    to judge how effective the method you used was in collecting reliable data.
b) Your conclusion,
    to judge how strong the evidence is that you have used to draw a conclusion.

Fertilisation
When sex cells join together to make a new individual, e.g. a sperm and an egg, or a pollen grain nucleus and an ovule nucleus.

Fetus
An embryo that has developed its main features, e.g. in humans after about 3 months.

Filtration
A process used to separate undissolved solids from liquids.

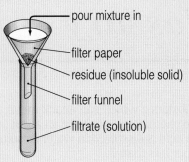

Food chain
A diagram that shows how food energy is passed between plants and animals.

Food web
A diagram that shows a number of food chains linked together.

Fossil fuels
A fuel made from the remains of plants and animals that died millions of years ago, e.g. coal, oil, natural gas.

Friction
A force when 2 surfaces rub together. It always pushes against the movement.

Fuel
A substance that is burned in air (oxygen) to give out energy.

Fuse
A safety device in an electrical circuit. It is a piece of wire that heats up and melts, breaking the circuit, if too much current passes through it.

Gas
A substance which is light, has the shape of its container and is easily squashed. The particles in a gas are far apart. They move quickly and in all directions.

Genes
Found in chromosomes, they control the inherited features of living things.

Gravity, gravitational force
A force of attraction between 2 objects.
The pull of gravity on you is your weight.

Habitat
The place where a plant or animal lives.

Herbivores
Animals that eat only plants.

Hibernate
To remain inactive throughout the winter months.

Inherited
The features that are passed on from parents to their offspring.

Independent variable (or input variable)
The factor that you choose to change in an investigation.

Indicator
A substance that changes colour depending on the pH of the solution you add it to.

Invertebrate
An animal without a backbone.

Kinetic energy
The energy of something which is moving.

Liquid
A substance which has the shape of its container, can be poured and is not easily squashed. The particles in a liquid are quite close together but free to move.

Melting point
The temperature at which a solid melts and changes into a liquid.

Migration
Moving from one place to another in different seasons to avoid adverse or harsh conditions.

Neutral
Something which is neither an acid nor an alkali.

Neutralisation
The chemical reaction of an acid with an alkali, in which they cancel each other out.

Non-renewable resources
Energy sources that are used up and not replaced, e.g. fossil fuels.

Nucleus of a cell
A round structure that controls the cell and contains the instructions to make more cells.

Orbit
The path of a planet or a satellite.
Its shape is usually an ellipse (oval).

Organ
A structure made up of different tissues that work together to do a particular job.

Organism
A living thing, such as a plant, an animal or a microbe.

Ovary
Where the eggs are made in a female.

Oviduct
A tube that carries an egg from the ovary to the uterus.

Parallel circuit
A way of connecting things in an electric circuit, so that the current divides and passes through different branches.

Period
When the lining of the uterus breaks down and blood and cells leave the body through the vagina.

pH number
A number which shows how strong an acid or alkali is. Acids have pH 0–6 (pH 0 is very strong acid). Alkalis have pH 8–14 (pH 14 is very strong alkali).

Placenta
A structure that forms in the uterus allowing the blood of the baby and the blood of the mother to come close together.

Pollination
The transfer of pollen from the anthers to the stigma of a flower.

Population
A group of animals or plants of the same species living in the same habitat.

Potential energy
Stored energy, e.g. a bike at the top of a hill has gravitational potential energy.

Prediction
A statement that describes and explains what you think will happen in an investigation.

Principle of conservation of energy
The amount of energy before a transfer is always equal to the amount of energy after the transfer. The energy is 'conserved'.

Producers
Green plants that make their own food by photosynthesis.

Product
A substance made as a result of a chemical reaction.

Proportional
The link between 2 variables, e.g. the extension of a spring is directly proportional to the load on it, so if you double the load, the extension is also doubled.

Puberty
The age at which the sexual organs become developed.

Reaction
A chemical change which makes a new substance.

Reliability
A measure of the trust you can put in your results. You can improve the reliability of your results by repeating readings and taking averages.

Renewable energy resources
Energy sources that do not get used up, e.g. solar energy, wind, waves, tides, etc.

Resistance
A thin wire gives more resistance to an electric current than a thick wire.

Respiration
The release of energy from food in our cells. Usually using up oxygen and producing carbon dioxide.

glucose + oxygen $\longrightarrow$ carbon dioxide + water + energy

Resultant force
The result of *unbalanced forces*. (See page 148).

Sample size
The number of subjects included in an enquiry.

Satellite
An object that goes round a planet or a star, e.g. the Moon goes round the Earth.

Saturated solution
A solution in which no more solute can dissolve at that temperature.

Series circuit
A way of connecting things in an electric circuit, so that the current flows through each one in turn.

Solar System
The Sun and all 9 planets that go round it.

Solid
A substance which has a fixed shape, is not runny and is not squashed easily. The particles in a solid are packed very closely together – they vibrate but do not move from place to place.

Soluble
Describes something which dissolves, e.g. salt is soluble in water.

Solute
The solid that dissolves to make a solution.

Solution
The clear liquid made when a solute dissolves in a solvent, e.g. salt (solute) dissolves in water (solvent) to make salt solution.

Solvent
The liquid that dissolves the solute to make a solution.

Species
A type of living thing that breeds and produces fertile offspring.

Speed
How fast an object is moving.

$$\text{Speed} = \frac{\text{distance travelled}}{\text{time taken}}$$

Sperm
Male sex cell.

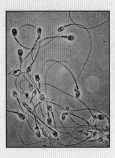

States of matter
The 3 states in which matter can be found: *solid*, *liquid* and *gas*.

Temperature
How hot or cold something is.
It is measured in °C, using a thermometer.

Testis
Where the sperms are made in a male.

Thermal energy
Another name for heat energy.

Thinking distance
The distance travelled in a car during the driver's reaction time.

Tissue
A group of similar cells that look the same and do the same job.

Transfer of energy
The movement of energy from one place to another, for a job to be done.

Transformation of energy
When energy changes from one form to another.

Unbalanced forces
If 2 forces do not cancel out each other, they are unbalanced. There will be a resultant force. The object will change its speed or change its direction.

Universal indicator
A liquid which changes colour when acids or alkalis are added to it. It shows whether the acid or alkali is strong or weak.

Upthrust
Upward force produced on an object in a liquid or a gas. There is a very small upthrust in a gas.

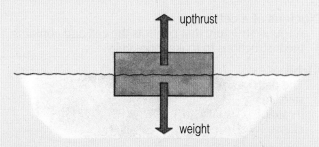

Uterus
The womb, where a fertilised egg settles and grows into a baby.

Vacuole
The space in a plant cell that is filled with a watery solution called cell sap.

Validity of conclusions
A measure of the trust you can have in your conclusions drawn from the data that you collected in your investigation.

Variable
The things (factors) that can change (or vary) in an investigation.

Variation
Differences between *different* species, e.g. between dogs and cats, or between individuals of the *same* species, e.g. people in your class.

Vertebrate
An animal that has a backbone.

Index